OPEN YOUR HEARTS

Open Your Hearts

THE STORY OF THE JEWISH WAR ORPHANS IN CANADA

Fraidie Martz

Véhicule Press

Published with the assistance of The Canada Council.

Cover: "Paris Transit, 1948," war orphans heading for Canada courtesy of Canadian Jewish Congress National Archives.

Typesetting by Simon Garamond.
Printing by Imprimerie d'Édition Marquis Ltée

Dépôt légal, Bibliothèque nationale du Québec
and National Library of Canada, fourth quarter 1996.

CANADIAN CATALOGUING IN PUBLICATION
Martz, Fraidie
Open your hearts : the story of the Jewish
war orphans in Canada

ISBN 1-55065-078-5

1. Jewish orphans Canada History—20th century.
2. World War, 1939-1945–Children. 3. Canada–
Emigration and immigration–History–20th century
I. Title

D810.C4M37 1966   971'.004924   C96-900461-3

Published by Véhicule Press, POB. 125, Place du Parc Station,
Montreal, Quebec, Canada H2W 2M9
http://www.cam.org/~vpress

Distributed by General Distribution Services
30 Lesmill Road, Don Mills, Ontario M3B 2T6
1-800-387-0172 or
4600 Witmer Industrial Estates #4, Niagara Falls, NY 14305
1-800-805-1083

Printed in Canada on alkaline paper.

DEDICATION

It was my privilege to have known Greta Fischer and Renate Wilson without whom I would never have written this book. It was Greta who introduced me to the story of the Jewish war orphans. Renate, accomplished author and adventurer, showed me that I could be the one to tell it. My friendship with these women, both refugees from Czechoslovakia who made their own way to creative and rich lives in Canada, left me profoundly changed. Greta and Renate both died in 1988, but they were with me through every phase of this project.

In the context of the history of World War II the story of the Jewish war orphans in Canada is small. The grandiose language of military victories and defeats does not apply. We seem to lack the terms to describe how goodness and trust are restored when the battles are over. The gradual triumph over despair which occurs in the warmth of a kitchen or by a comforting hand on a child falling asleep, does not interest the traditional historian. Little is known about the hundreds of men and women who helped the young people orphaned by war realign their shattered lives. I dedicate this book to them as well.

Contents

ACKNOWLEDGEMENTS

9

PREFACE

I I

CHAPTER ONE

Pier 21: The Kids Arrive

I 7

CHAPTER TWO

Permission Granted–At Last

2 7

CHAPTER THREE

The Rules of the Game

39

CHAPTER FOUR

Gearing Up in Canada

5 5

CHAPTER FIVE

The Search in Europe

7 6

CHAPTER SIX

Arrival and Reception

108

CHAPTER SEVEN

Other People's Houses

118

CHAPTER EIGHT

Fitting In

153

CHAPTER NINE

Looking Back

165

EPILOGUE

177

NOTES

185

Acknowledgements

The Wilson family has a special place in my gratitude. My first and greatest thanks go to Andrew Wilson. His gift as a writer and editor drew a map for me of a sphere that I had not known existed. Without his encouragement, critiques and praise, the idea for this book would have been but another of my many daydreams. He knew how to assuage my doubts and spent untold hours giving me invaluable tutorials.

Jim Wilson, husband of Renate and father of Andrew, a civil engineer and a professor emeritus of Urban and Regional Planning, taught me the principles of organization and how to build a solid structure.

I wish also to thank Janice Rosen, Archivist of the Canadian Jewish Congress National Archives and her staff; the many librarians of the Vancouver Public Library for their co-operation and help; and Marilla B. Guptil, Chief, Archives Unit of the United Nations Archives for providing documentation on the UNRRA.

Dr. Robert Krell at the University of British Columbia, always ready to share his many thoughts and insights, introduced me to the network of child survivors across the country.

My husband Sam and my daughters Julie, Carol, and Lisa, taught me by example that I could accomplish whatever I set out to do, regardless of the age at which I began.

Finally, I wish to express my deepest thanks to all the survivors too numerous to mention by name, who responded to my call with the utmost generosity. They gave me a profound appreciation of their struggles, and knowing them has enriched my life.

If you remain
I will still be alive
as the pit of the plum
contains in itself the tree
the nest and the bird
and all else besides

—Abraham Sutzkever

Preface

THE ARRIVAL OF LEON FRIEDMAN brought everything to a sudden stop in our classroom that snowy winter day in 1947. The war had ended what felt like decades earlier; the names and faces of older brothers reported missing or killed in action already blurred. By then I had only a faint memory of the long walks home at the end of the school day, steeled for news about some new disaster from the front during the uncertain years of the early 1940s.

The snow fell so heavily that from my desk in the middle row of the grade nine classroom, the window looked as though it had been plastered clumsily with gobs of white paint. It was hard to concentrate on the class lesson knowing how tough it would be getting home through the snowdrifts and the cold. In the fading light my cheerless public high school with its pretentious name, Strathcona Academy, felt momentarily hospitable; and for once I was in no hurry for the school day to end.

The school principal, an austere, authoritarian man whom we all feared and viewed only from a distance at school ceremonies, came to the door at the front of the class. Trailing a few steps behind him was a neatly dressed boy with an extremely pale face. He looked thin and small compared to us and it was impossible to stop ourselves from staring as he stood in the bright doorway. With all eyes turned on him, he walked with bowed head down the aisle to the desk assigned him at the back of the classroom.

I knew nothing about Leon Friedman, save that he was Jewish, fifteen years old, had come to Montreal from Poland, and had somehow survived the Holocaust and the Second World War. And yet, I felt I knew all about him, having lived with his shadow for most of my young life.

Ever since I could remember—and long before the war—I had been awakened from sleep by my parents' agitated talk, always in Yiddish or Romanian, about the terrible things that were happening to fellow Jews in Europe. By speaking of these things in their mother tongues, or only behind closed doors, my mother and father believed they could shield me from their fears; but every word that travelled through my bedroom wall nevertheless carried that fear. From week to week pale blue airmail envelopes, the only personal letters we ever received, arrived describing the worsening conditions in Europe. Pages and pages of dense script, written with perfect penmanship on the thinnest paper I had ever seen, told about a life of terror. With each letter my parents' mood grew more sombre; and as they read them aloud the words seemed to suck the colour off the walls. One letter among many stands out in my memory. Written by a father from Europe sometime in 1938, this is what it said: "In great distress and desperation our family appeals to you for help. If no assistance comes we shall all go under. Please help and save us. You are our last hope. We are very modest, have perfect manners and originate from a very old and esteemed family. If I cannot immigrate myself I humbly beg that at least you can get my children a permit."

From the letters that gave detailed and graphic accounts, I was able to picture the events clearly. Everywhere, the writers said, they saw Jewish people like themselves brutally beaten, or taken away and never seen again. It was dangerous to venture into the streets; it was not safe to remain at home. Mothers and fathers feared for their lives and those of their children. These images crowded insistently into my mind as I sat watching life on the street from our front room window. They clung to me as I watched ballgames being played or skipping ropes whipping the air on the last green field remaining on the street. They were everywhere.

I listened to these stories of terror at an age when other children were being told fairy tales, which I could not bear to hear. All fictional dangers were intolerable because they merged in my mind with the true stories I was hearing.

One day in the autumn of 1939—it was one of those sweltering Montreal days you thought had retreated with the summer—a family with a name I had not heard before moved into a house just two doors away. Up to that time nobody had ever moved onto our clean and tidy street suddenly, without the usual advance talk from someone in the neighbourhood. I guessed this connected in some way, how I could not say, with the letters. This was not the first time a new family had moved in about whom no one knew anything: what made them unusual was that no mover's truck came to unload furniture and household goods and give us watching children clues about the new family entering our domain. In place of these clues I substituted fragments of the stories and letters I had heard and every time I passed the flat I walked faster. The house had already been marked by misfortune. The mother of the family who had lived there had recently died and that made me all the more fearful of its interior. But there was no blocking it out because all the flats on our side of the street had identical layouts. The Gewurz's house—for that was the name of the new family—was exactly the same as ours. It could well have been our house and the thought made me shudder.

By the time I entered McGill in 1950 I understood the words of many authors about how all Jews of this generation are "a kind of survivor." I knew that I was not rounded up with other Jews by the Nazis or forced into cattle cars and taken to Dachau, only because my parents had managed to immigrate to Canada at an earlier time— before Canada's borders closed.

Helen Poznansky (not her real name) had not been as fortunate. Early in the first term, when I was quite lost in the depths of Professor Duthie's exegesis of Shakespeare's tragedies delivered from a distant podium in McGill University's Moyse Hall, I surfaced briefly to wonder how my fellow students were faring. Something drew me to notice Helen. She always came alone, spoke to no one and left the moment the class ended as though in a great hurry, while the rest of us stood around chatting. By chance, I overheard her say a few words to the person sitting in front of her, and recognized her Polish accent. I was reminded of Leon.

In time I succeeded in striking an acquaintance with Helen and learned that she too had come to Canada as a war orphan in the care of Canadian Jewish Congress. Working as a waitress at night and living in a cheap room, she was managing to attend McGill with the help of a meagre subsidy from Congress. At the time, I was living at home with my widowed mother in a spacious house, the very house that had remained closed to the desperate call for homes when Congress was given permission to bring the war orphans to Canada. Was it too late I wondered? I tried to befriend Helen, but didn't know how to begin and never succeeded. Nothing in our pasts or immediate circumstances, I suspected, equipped us with a handle to form a friendship.

Four years later I entered McGill's School of Social Work, and met a woman who made a strong impression on me. In the wood-panelled study of a converted turn-of-the-century Victorian mansion on University Avenue, Greta Fischer watched us, her younger classmates, seat ourselves hesitantly around the table. She scrutinized us with more kindly authority than the lecturer seated at the head of the table. Her dark hair, peppered with grey and drawn neatly into a bun at the nape of her neck, contrasted with her sparkling, lively eyes. But it was the open-hearted way she laughed with her conspicuously uneven front teeth in full display, that added the final touch to what struck me as the kind of beauty and majesty possessed by someone who had taken part in momentous events.

I soon learned that Greta had been refused entry into the School of Social Work twice, and it was only by chance that on her third and final attempt she was accepted. The system had no way to evaluate her pre-war studies in Czechoslovakia; no way to gauge her work in helping to rehabilitate children at United Nations Relief and Rehabilitation Administration's International Children's Centre outside of Dachau from 1945 until 1947; and no record of her contribution to the adjustment of the war orphans allowed into Canada.

During lunch breaks and in free periods, Greta's compelling stories about "those days" poured out in torrents. There was never time enough to tell it well, she would lament, and unfailingly ended by saying, "The children's stories must be written for the world to know what happened in those terrible times." And I thought then—Greta's work with the "unaccompanied children" as they were called, and the principles that guided her should have been an integral component of every class on child welfare.

Three decades later I stood facing the door of Greta's Jerusalem apartment at 18 Hapalmach Street; a door completely covered with children's drawings. Recovering from a massive heart attack, Greta knew that her life was nearing its end, and greeted me by repeating what she had so often and so long ago said, but now with much greater urgency: "The children's story must be told."

The work began collaboratively with Greta in Jerusalem, and me in Vancouver. Since her death in 1988 I have carried on in the hope that she would have approved of the direction the work has taken. Greta would have wished to be remembered, I believe, simply as one member of a remarkable group of people who made a contribution to restoring sanity and love to the world. She would also have wanted to leave a record of how the child survivors of the Holocaust learned to live in Canadian society with confidence and hope, and how Canadians participated with open hearts towards this end.

It is for Greta, and for Leon and Helen, and the other players in this drama that I have collected the stories of the children and those people in Europe and in Canada who played significant roles in helping rebuild their lives. It is a story with many noble dimensions. I hope I have told it with the merit it deserves.

CHAPTER ONE

Pier 21: The Kids Arrive

ON SEPTEMBER 15, 1947 a heavy fog pressed down on the buildings of downtown Halifax, appearing to make them all the same height, filling in the empty spaces between so that one could barely see where one building ended and another began, leaching the colour from their red brick and painted wood walls. As the day came to a close the fading light, diffused by the moist air, made the fog seem ever thicker.

At the waterfront in the south end of the city stood a large, two-storey immigration building with barred windows. Pier 21 was the first glimpse of the country for the immigrants who poured ashore over the years. Its resemblance to a prison on the outside was even more pronounced inside. Large wire cages lined the back wall of the huge dark hall, and were intended not for forcible confinement but to speed up processing. Disturbed by the impression they knew it made on already nervous immigrants, the Pier's staff had made many attempts over the years to have the cages removed, but with no success. The front portion of the reception hall was not much more welcoming. A huge Union Jack looked down imperiously on the rows and rows of wooden benches lining the highly polished floors.

Pier 21's grimness was softened only by the groups of Halifax citizens who came to welcome the new immigrants as they came off the ships. The welcoming tradition was one of long standing, having begun in 1768 when a group of Scottish settlers formed the North British Society.[1] By the turn of the twentieth century, volunteer groups representing the major Christian churches, as well as the Halifax Jewish community, could always be counted on to meet the ships. But on this Monday in September 1947, the crowd included a group of ten middle-aged men and women who had come to Pier 21 on a special mission.

Each person in that group was dressed simply, the women in skirts and blouses, the men in clothes they wore to work. This was no time to pay attention to something as trivial as appearance, as if it mattered. But they knew it could matter. Everything they did, however trifling in another context, might have enormous significance.

In silence, they stood close together in a tidy formation glancing at one another as if needing encouragement. Clearly they were not members of one family—no arms interlocked, no hands on shoulders in the intimate way of families awaiting a momentous arrival. And there were no children among them. Yet the way they looked at one another indicated some complicity or shared purpose. The odd word was exchanged, not because something needed to be said, but to give a feeling of reality to the event that was about to unfold. They had spent too many years picturing themselves standing together in Pier 21, as they now did, to fully believe the reality of the scene before them.

What had brought them here on this day? Each remembered with great clarity the chilling words sent out across the country in bulletins from Canadian Jewish Congress headquarters in Montreal.

There is a Jewish child, in a European DP camp, who is waiting for you to let him begin to live.

He is leaving behind him a nightmare of death and ashes…yet he is optimistic, cheerful, full of the hope of youth. He is the child for whom your heart bled when you read the news of Nazi *schrecklichkeit* a few years back … Today, no longer anonymous, no longer separated from your succour by an ocean, he stands at your very doorstep, needing a home, a family, the love and guidance of a father and mother.

You want to help this child, from the bottom of your heart.

Is there room in your home for him—a place in the warmth
of your family circle for which his heart is so hungry?
If there's room in your heart, there's room in your home.[2]

The horrors of which the world had known only in whispers and
sporadic reports during the war years had long since been revealed to
the people of Canada by journalists and photographers. Only two years
earlier, at the time of liberation, the front pages of newspapers and
newsreels had seared into everyone's mind horrific images never before seen in the history of humankind. The photographs of piles of
corpses in mass graves and emaciated survivors wearing striped rags
behind the barbed wire fences of the concentration camps had left
indelible marks on everyone's memory.

Many of the children about to come ashore had witnessed these
unspeakable events with their own eyes. They had seen their parents
beaten and murdered, and had themselves been systematically
terrorized and publicly spurned. No one in the waiting crowd could
know if these young people would ever recover from their experiences
despite everyone's best and kindest efforts. The men and women
waiting in Pier 21 struggled with these thoughts as they prepared to
open their arms to the new arrivals.

This day was the culmination of years of work by groups scattered
all across the country. For years meetings had been held in people's
homes, first to figure out a strategy to obtain government permission,
later to plan the details for this day and the weeks to follow. The endless
letters written and answered, the search for people ready to help, the
assignment of roles and responsibilities—all of that was now in the
past. Differences of opinion had been thrashed out in emotional
debates. All that needed to be said had been said; all that had to be
done was now done. But no one could be sure of having prepared well
enough. Nothing could stop people from worrying that small things,
so important in conveying first impressions, might not have been
considered—or even whether the right decisions had been made about
major issues. No amount of preparation could overcome their

apprehensions about unknowable expectations and needs. And there was no way to stop them from wishing, irrational as they knew it to be, that landing on Canadian soil would bring the newcomers a complete break with the past—wipe the slate clean and enable them to begin all over again.

These men and women had taken their places in the pier long before the ship was expected, so as not to miss a first sight of the ship as it entered the harbour with its long-awaited passengers. Now they watched tensely as the huge hawsers tied the S.S.Aquitania to land and the gangway was lowered after its ten-day trip across the stormy North Atlantic from Bremerhaven. Among the long procession of 850 immigrant passengers making their way to shore along the open ramp connecting ship to pier were sixteen boys and four girls, ranging in age from eleven to eighteen. Arriving direct from displaced camps in Germany they were the first of 1,123 orphaned young survivors of the Holocaust to arrive in Canada.

The arrival was given no special attention by the general public in Halifax, and was entered into the port's records in the usual terse official code. And when the twenty youngsters, who had been assigned homes in Montreal arrived there two days later, the Montreal *Gazette* carried only a short item conveying no sense of the human victory, or the race against time and the battle against red tape, which made it possible for these youngsters to be in Canada now. Beneath a photograph of teenaged Anita "enjoying her first ice cream" the article's opening sentences read:

> Twenty Jewish war orphans, who survived the Nazi reign of terror in Europe and choose to come to Canada rather than return to their native land, arrived at Montreal Airport last night on two T.C.A. flights from Halifax to start their badly disrupted lives anew in this "land of promise."
>
> Eager-eyed and full of pep despite their long trip the young-sters said they were glad they had finally arrived, and looked

forward happily to the chance of becoming Canadian citizens.

All slated for Montreal homes, the orphans, ranging in age from 10 to 18, will either carry on with their education or go to work.

The Toronto Daily Star, on the other hand, chose to report the event by printing a column from the *Jewish Chronicle* of Milwaukee praising the Canadian Project.

> *Canada Shows the Way* ... Admittedly, 1,000 orphans isn't much for a big country like Canada. The country could absorb many more—not only children but adults. However, these 1,000 children are enough to show how little the U.S. is doing in the same direction. By contrast this country has been pursuing a policy that is comparatively heartless. Except for a few children allowed to come here for adoption we have not inaugurated any general policy on behalf of these homeless waifs.

Only those people waiting at the dock that day will have seen the short boy, his eyes filled with tears, walk to shore clutching a rolled-up Hebrew prayer shawl and a shattered pair of glasses. They were the mementos of his father's death. In the concentration camp when the Nazis discovered that the father's glasses were broken and therefore he was no longer useful as a labourer, they had shot him.[3]

Among those waiting on the dock was Joseph Kage, the young director of the Montreal Jewish community's summer Sunshine Camp. In early July he had received a telephone call from Louis Zuker, an esteemed community leader in the Jewish Immigrant Aid Society (JIAS), asking him to outline a plan for the reception of the young survivors. This he did. About a week later, Kage was asked to join the JIAS staff to carry out his plan; when he hesitated, they assured him that it was likely to be a short-term assignment, perhaps for a few months, a year at the most—not to worry, it would not interfere with his ambition to advance to a faculty position at the McGill School of Social Work. As it turned out, Dr. Kage soon became the National Executive Director of JIAS and directed its operations for forty-five years. By the time of his retirement, he had established a national reputation as an authority on immigration, as well as making a name for himself as a Yiddish scholar, teacher and translator.

Joseph Kage still lives on de l'Epée Avenue, only a few blocks away from the Reception Home where the Holocaust orphans lived when they first arrived in Montreal. Asked about that foggy September day almost a half-century before, he spoke quietly and carefully, each word measured for accuracy before being allowed to cross his lips, in the character of the meticulous translator.

> In Halifax I met with the local reception committee headed by the stalwart Noah Heinish. As I proceeded to the boat to meet the children my anxiety mounted. Many thoughts flooded through my mind—the sacrifice of Isaac; Tisha B'Av; Torquemada; the massacres of Tach V'tat; the pogroms in Czarist Russia; and a vision of a mountain of two million shoes, shoes that belonged to the million Jewish children killed by the Nazis.
>
> Here I was to face a group of children who had lost everything and everybody, who had been hunted physically, were emotionally deprived, incarcerated and tortured—children of the Holocaust. What should be my first greeting? What should I tell them? The Halifax reception committee was ready to welcome them with comforts, but this would not solve the basic problem of 'breaking the ice.' I tried to recollect the various social work interviewing techniques and approaches, but they all seemed empty, cold and inappropriate.
>
> As I boarded the boat something welled up in me and all of a sudden I knew the less said the better. The only valid greeting

War orphans (and others) wearing tags in reception area,
Halifax harbour, 1948.
Canadian Jewish Congress National Archives

was the age-long basic precept in Jewish tradition. As I reached the group of youngsters who were waiting for me I introduced myself, shook each one's hand and simply said 'Sholom Aleichem, Baruch Habah' (peace unto you, bless your arrival). I knew they understood me and I knew that they knew what I meant.

How do the children, on the other hand, remember the arrival? Interviewed today, some remember high spirits and a mindless optimism. Their lives were beginning again, and the walk down the ship's gangplank was the first set of steps in those new lives.

In this excerpt from Leslie Mezei's journal which is attached to his immigration documents in Congress archives, he records his impressions of the ocean voyage and his arrival in Canada.

The big ship is ready to leave the harbour of Bremen. The ropes are slowly drawn up, the big muddy anchor is pulled up with a great roar. The ship slowly pulls away from the shore and everyone makes a big sigh.

As I look about I see many faces shining and they all tell a unique story. The boy on my right looks as if he never knew what food was, the girl beside him is wearing torn rags.

The ship is something like heaven to us, the eleven days of travel went by fast. They were the dawn of our new life.

After a brief check at the immigration office we were given a big reception. Smiling women greet us and overwhelm us with everything we desire. They tell us how good it will be for us.

After a couple of hours we are on a train. We feel a big freedom— nobody asks us for identification and we get everything we want. A day later we reach Montreal. The city looks alive because everything is lit with cars and people moving on the street. This is not anything like the dead city, Munchen. After a grand reception we are given our rooms in our temporary home at the Reception Centre. There we have a good, peaceful rest.

Others could not shake off the horror of their recent past. Joseph Rothbart, now the long-time director of Mt. Sinai Hospital in Montreal (previously Ste. Agathe, Quebec) was then a sixteen-year-old, Romanian concentration camp survivor. This is how he recalls the arrival:

The *S.S. Aquitania* reached the harbour as dark was falling, or maybe it was the thick fog that made me think it was evening. From the ship at anchor I saw on the shore what looked like a misshapen sphere of light so blinding it paralyzed me with fear. The broken flashes of light coming away from it and darting in all directions from—as I learned later—the moving cars made the scene the more terrifying. Remember, in war-torn Europe we had no electricity, and certainly no cars, so that the nights were black and no buildings lit. I was too scared to leave the ship. I was convinced that I would be absorbed by this glaring enormity. I hid as far away as I could get—deep down in the ship's boiler room. I heard the Canadian officials and members of the Canadian Jewish community take my fellow passengers to shore and the confusion that broke out after they discovered they were one person short.

When they returned aboard with two RCMP officers in uniform to look for the missing person I was convinced they had come to execute me. With the captain's help they eventually found me. The grotesque lights of the city, my inability to speak the language, the worry about how I would earn my living, turned me into a helpless knot of rope like the coils I saw lying inert on the wooden deck. I was paralyzed with fear.

When Joseph arrived on shore and had passed through the immigration formalities, he could hardly believe that the waiting people handed him some pocket money to spend on the train did he begin to accept their sincerity. But even more significant, beyond receiving attention and generosity, was understanding he had the right to choose where in Canada he wanted to go. Forty long years later, the memory of those gifts of freedom and choice brought a flush of colour to his cheeks and a boyish grin to his countenance.

Most of the war orphans were overwhelmed by the warmth of their initial reception in Canada. The men and women waiting their arrival embraced them lovingly and then showered them with parcels of food, candy, and fruit.

Later, the orphans were taken on a tour of the city and invited to private homes for meals. Local merchants presented each of them with a winter overcoat; theatre owners gave them free passes, while Jewish and non-Jewish students at Dalhousie University threw a party for them and gave them more gifts.

Though the arrival of the first twenty Holocaust orphans was the beginning of their lives as Canadians, it is actually the mid-point of our story, and we will meet the two Josephs again, as was well as others who arrived at Pier 21. But to understand how they got there, as well as what happened to them in the days and years that followed, we have to look back a few decades.

CHAPTER TWO

Permission Granted—At Last

TEN DAYS for the *S.S. Aquitania* to cross the North Atlantic from Bremerhaven to Halifax; but fourteen years to navigate the turbulent waters of Canadian immigration policy to get permission for that voyage.

Beginning in the thirties following Hitler's rise to power, the Jewish community pressed the government in every way possible to allow refugees into the country.[1] Discrimination against the Jew was achieved not through the exercise of powers, but rather through the abuse of powers. Canada's immigration department was in the hands of Frederick Blair, an avowed anti-semite, who personally scrutinized each application to decide its eligibility. Working with the single-minded purpose of refusing entry to any Jewish refugee, he rejected every Jewish applicant.

Problems of immigration called up a vast pool of collective history, but offered few guides to the task of persuading government to change immigration restrictions against Jewish families seeking entry to Canada. Across the country, in business offices and boardrooms, in the halls and around cluttered desks of community organizations, in clothing factories and food shops, in poor homes and affluent ones— Jewish people of all political stripes and walks of life came together to debate how to change government policy. A number of the non-Jewish leaders of the Canadian National Committee on Refugees also joined the cause.

The community was far from well-financed, organized or united.

Dissent and divisions flourished. At first Canadian Jews, most of whom were immigrants unsure of their political place and uneasy in the world of domestic power brokerage, looked to their three Jewish members of parliament—Samuel Jacobs (Montreal, Liberal), Sam Factor (Toronto, Liberal) and A.A. Heaps (Winnipeg, CCF)—to moderate government policy on immigration and refugees. When these members failed to win even the smallest concession in Ottawa, the myth of their influence in the corridors of power died. Their failure put the refugee campaign in the hands of the Canadian Jewish Congress.

Established in 1919 as the democratic decision-making body within the Canadian Jewish community, Congress is recognized as the parliament and voice of Canadian Jewry to government and the outside world. The idea behind the organization was to co-ordinate, on a national basis, efforts to cope effectively and judiciously with internal and external problems. It was the only organization which could call upon all the Jewish community to unite. In its acceptance by almost all Canadian Jews and Jewish organizations, it has no counterpart in the country. Starting out as a sub-society of an immigrant group featuring dozens of ideologies and organizations, each with its own leaders and activists, it had grown into a dazzling complex of synagogues, health services, *landsmannschaften* (mutual benefit societies often organized by people from the same region in Europe), and others. A major contributing factor was the homogeneity of the Canadian Jewish population, in contrast with the U.S. where rifts had developed between successive immigrant groups. Except for the handful of early settlers, nearly all the Jews in Canada came from Eastern Europe.

From its earliest days Congress was concerned with immigration as well as safeguarding the civil, political, and religious rights of Jews. However, by the 1930s it had almost disappeared. In the relatively peaceful and unthreatening 1920s its founding impetus seemed unncessary. Congress was revived only when the rise of Nazism threatened the relatives of virtually every Jew in the country. At the same time anti-Jewish articles appeared in Quebec's influential newspapers, *Le Devoir* and *l'Action Catholique*; while in August 1933 the largest and most violent riot in Toronto's history occurred at Christie Pits baseball diamond when a banner emblazoned with a swastika was unfurled to enrage the Jewish team and its supporters.[2] These incidents, and others of similar intent, put Congress on the alert. But it wasn't until 1934 in reaction to a mass meeting convened by the journalist André Laurendeau in Montreal to protest a Jewish demonstration against Hitler that a Jewish Committee of "Forty-One" took action and the national Canadian Jewish Congress was resurrected.

The dangers could best be faced, it was believed, by marshalling all communal, financial and human resources in one national organization. The revival of Congress not only unified Canadian Jewry into one national community, it also supplied the newly established nation-wide Jewish community with an effective public forum. By 1938 Congress had established a semi-autonomous refugee organization.

Efforts to change government immigration policy preoccupied everyone: businesses, synagogues, clubs, and of course, Jewish homes. I suspect my family's house was typical of hundreds across the nation during the mid-1930s. Like many others in the neighbourhood, our house always had people coming and going at the end of the day to talk about immigration and European Jewry. At the first ring of the doorbell the kitchen table was whipped clear of the supper plates and whatever aromas were left over from supper were soon banished by the smoke from the men's cigarettes and cigars, and the clamour of inflamed voices. No one seemed to notice that the black chipped edges of the white enamel table top, always compulsively covered with a cloth when guests arrived, were left exposed. They looked as unashamed and defiant as the loud words which bounced off them.

The men and women who squeezed tight around the table argued non-stop about the merits of one tactic over another, critically analyzed and re-analyzed every word reported from official meetings, and deplored all the arguments and moves left out. To my young eyes, they never seemed to need to stop to draw breath. There was seldom agreement about anything, not even between my parents. Everybody was critical of the others. Sometimes a point was identified which reminded them of the reserved, polite approach adopted by the Canadian Jewish Congress. This would inevitably set off a shouting match between those who agreed with Congress' patient strategy and those who decried Congress as weak and ineffectual and demanded a more aggressive strategy like protesting in the streets.

Reality could no longer be ignored. After using all possible channels—repeated pressure on government in written and oral briefs, educational programs directed at public opinion on radio and in the press—much sympathy was produced but little action. With every failed effort rage burst out and flowed in all directions. As so often happens when the big issues can't be resolved, unimportant details took on an exaggerated significance and "magical thinking" (as psychologists would name it) produced some strange equations. "If Mr. J. had talked to Mr. A., instead of Mr. L. on Monday rather than on Friday, in Montreal rather than Ottawa, the outcome would have been different."

The voice I liked best was my mother's. When it was reported that the entreaties made cap-in-hand to Ottawa by Samuel Bronfman, mover and shaker of men and communities, had been turned down once again, she declared that, given the opportunity, *she* would know how to open Canada's closed gates. I loved her words and was convinced she could. At the same time, I sensed she believed there was some secret knowledge about the workings of this country that eluded her because she was a naturalized citizen rather than native-born, or maybe because of her accented, imperfect English. As her Canadian-born daughter I often wondered what gift I possessed that might help her. The only thing I could think of was correcting her English grammar, which I knew embarrassed her.

About one subject there was *never* any disagreement. A way had to be found to help rescue European sisters, brothers, and cousins. As immigrants themselves from not many years earlier, my parents and their friends felt supremely lucky. The haphazardness of their luck, they felt, bound them to the unlucky ones with a tight cord of obligation. My parents and their *landsmen* and *landswomen* were determined to find a way to rescue their kin.

A point was reached during these kitchen-table battles—and I could usually sense it coming—when the combatants ran out of energy. That became the moment for the storytellers to begin. Taking as much time as they needed, and giving every portion of their story equal weight, they told how they and their fellows had escaped from their tormentors in Eastern Europe when they were young. They couldn't be hurried, and no one ever dared to interrupt. Every step taken, every obstacle overcome—there was no such thing as a minor issue or insignificant detail—was related as if it had all happened the day before. Over and over again with very rare variations in these monotonous repetitions, the stories were told with great emotion and listened with rapt attenton. It occurred to me that everyone listened not for what was related, but rather for what might have been accidently left out in the repeated telling. It hadn't dawned on me then that the storytellers and their listeners were probably sifting for clues that could be weighed, measured and transformed into tools that might be used to open the sealed valve of immigration.

Even before the outbreak of war Congress had petitioned the government repeatedly for permission to bring displaced European children to Canada. Its appeals were refused, even though Congress had guaranteed that the Jewish community would support and care for the children. The government's main objection was that some of the children might have surviving parents and this would create intolerable pressure to bring their families, who would then seek to become landed immigrants, a possibility unacceptable to the Canadian government at that time. An additional argument for refusal was that the laws regarding the adoption and care of children were matters within the jurisdiction of the provinces. Despite this the Canadian

Government welcomed 6,000 British children in the first two years of the war and was ready to accept thousands of others.

When the Nazis tightened their hold on Vichy in 1942, the French government began rounding up Jews and deporting them to the East. Parents were forced to leave their sons and daughters behind in the internment camps where they too remained in immediate danger of deportation. Congress brought the tragedy of the approximately 5,000 children, aged two to fifteen, to the attention of the Canadian Government with new urgency and petitioned for help in the rescue of at least some of them.

It took a great deal of effort to convince the government that Congress had asked for asylum for children, not for their parents—almost all of whom had been deported. With this promise and the assurance that the Jewish community would assume full support for all the refugee children, permission was granted on October 2, 1942 to bring five hundred of these children from France to Canada, with the understanding that an additional five hundred might be authorized at a later date.

This permission was granted but not without major misgivings. Frederick Blair, director of the Immigration Branch of the Department of Mines and Resources, did not hesitate to voice his objections about the enterprise. (Note that immigration at that time was in the portfolio of the Department of Mines and Resources.) He told his minister, Thomas Crerar, that the Jewish community would find it very difficult to look after one thousand children satisfactorily: "Regular welfare organizations have expressed criticism a number of times of the Jewish method of handling earlier movements."[3] One is hard-pressed to comprehend what "movements" are referred to since in the past only one group of Jewish war orphans from the Ukraine had been allowed into the country. Likely, this is the mark left by one of the country's most prominent social workers, Charlotte Whitton, who had an influential voice in Ottawa. Not only did she send memorandums to welfare councils throughout the country warning of the problems inherent in admitting non-British, i.e. Jewish, refugee children, but she followed this with a cross-country tour speaking directly to provincial child welfare authorities.

There was another reason for Congress to feel a precariousness in the permission granted. For political reasons, Ottawa had asked that its decision be given no publicity. It was understood that it was necessary to keep the decision quiet for fear that Quebec would attempt to have it reversed, as it had succeeded in doing with previous schemes to bring refugees into the country. Saul Hayes therefore warned Jewish community leaders that publicity might kill the plan. But there was no way to keep word from spreading when everyone knew that this was the last opportunity to save a loved one from the murderous hands of the Nazis.

Plans were underway at once to find homes, schools and other services for the one thousand children. Two ships were chartered, doctors and nurses chosen, and social workers were given "crash courses" in the problems they might encounter among the children. In Irving Abella's words, "The enthusiasm and energy of Canadian Jewry, so long pent up while waiting on something to do, now burst forth. Everyone, it seemed, was ready to act, if only a handful of Jewish children could be saved."[4]

By November 1942, the children had been brought together and were waiting in Marseilles for the ships to take them to safety. It was at that moment that the Allies began their invasion of North Africa, and the Nazis tightened their grip on Vichy. The rescue operation failed and the children were never seen again. David Rome, Congress historian, insists that the Canadian government would surely have known about the impending invasion when they advised Congress to gather the children in Marseilles. He questions the sincerity of the government's goodwill. Canadian Jewry was staggered by the shock.

Other ways had to be found to make some dent in immigration policy. Congress turned for advice on strategy to one of its few friends within the bureaucracy. Norman Robertson, the politically shrewd assistant under-secretary of state for External Affairs talking off the record to Saul Hayes, executive director of Congress couldn't have been more blunt when he said:

> The Jewish community can obtain something only if a sufficient pressure be exerted. A brief to be effective must cite chapter and verse of what other countries have done in the matter of alleviating the human distress of refugees. The humanitarian side will not move the government to the same degree as the factual story of the numbers taken by the U.S., U.K., and other countries.[5]

When the war ended, the government's attitude didn't change; Jewish displaced persons desperate to leave Europe were still barred from entering Canada despite persistent requests from concerned relatives for special consideration through orders-in-council. Such applications became part of the collective battle to open the country to refugees, and the one lever Canadian Jews had. But sending an application was mainly a symbolic act—few were granted—and flooding Ottawa with applications was a desperate manoeuvre born of diminishing options. A.L. Joliffe, Director of Immigration, complained in October of 1945 to the undersecretary of External Affairs that "the department is literally flooded with appeals from residents of Canada to arrange for the admission of relatives."[6]

The bureaucracy's resistence to opening Canada's doors was matched by that of a large segment of the Canadian public. In January 1946, Brooke Claxton, Minister of National Health and Welfare, had reported to Jack Pickersgill, Special Assistant to the Prime Minister, "The people are getting steamed up about the government taking in the waifs and strays of Europe."[7]

Nonetheless, in March 1946, signs of a change of climate became apparent. An interdepartmental committee struck by External Affairs met with representatives from that department, as well as from

Immigration, Labour, and Health and Welfare. The committee reviewed the pro-refugee pressure coming not only from Canadian Jews but also the international community. Goaded by External Affairs it agreed to recommend to Cabinet that Canada should begin to admit some refugees. However, the agreement specified that the new terms be couched in the form of a special program based on orders-in-council, rather than a wholesale change in policy or the Immigration Act itself.

As word of the proposed changes filtered out to the community it generated a great deal of excitement, but also caused much worry. The community leaders feared, not surprisingly, that advance public-ity might upset the government and cause it to change its plans. Hopes had been dashed too many times for anybody to doubt that any flimsy excuse could cancel a lifting of restrictions. But rumours could not be contained and expectations continued to skyrocket until it became known that Joliffe had recommended that first-degree relatives spon-sored by Canadian relatives be permitted to enter the country.

An order-in-council was finally issued in May 1946 by J.A. Glen, Minister responsibile for Immigration. On the surface the order seemed generous, but the fine print proved it to be anything but. A first-degree relative was very narrowly defined and the order made no special mention of refugees or displaced persons. Only a small number of previously barred family members would find it possible to enter Canada, and it was unclear when even these few would be able to come. No provisions were made for transporting or for establishing refugee processing facilties in Europe. In addition, neither the Jewish community as a whole nor individual religious or community organizations were permitted to act as corporate bodies in sponsoring refugees. There was good reason to be suspicious and disheartened. Nothing was to change for a whole year.

Still, pressures were mounting from the international community and from Canadian officials working in External Affairs in Europe. A core of young, progressive and well-educated personnel, often more open-minded on the refugee issue than those in the Immigration

Branch, found themselves in the distasteful position of defending the Canadian policy, of which they were critical. Moreover, Georges Vanier, the Canadian ambassador to France, who was deeply affected by the plight of refugees in that country and whose embassy in Paris was beseiged by appeals requesting permission to join relatives in Canada, appealed repeatedly to Ottawa for an easing of restrictions. It was obvious, at least to External Affairs, that in order to avoid suffering an "international black eye" immigration authorities and the cabinet had best change their position.

In the same month Charity Grant, a member of a Canadian team of the United Nations Relief and Rehabilitation Administration (UNRRA) in Europe, added her voice urging a policy change in a letter to Brooke Claxton, Minister of Health and Welfare:

> I wish Canada would offer to take a group of Jewish children. So far no country has offered any permanent haven to any of them. Canada says it must play the part of a major power. Well let her show herself. Let her be the first to offer refuge to some of these children. We have here thousands of orphans all of whom have no place to go. I can't tell you what it would mean to thousands of people to think that at long last one country had offered to take even a small group of children. I would absolutely burst with pride if Canada were to offer a home to some of Hitler's victims. It would be a magnificent gesture.[8]

As well as this humanitarian pressure, forces from within the country were asking for a re-evaluation of its labour needs.

In early February 1947 came an auspicious sign of a turnabout in government policy. MacKenzie King, who up until then had kept himself at arm's length from the debate, at last agreed to meet with a small delegation from Canadian Jewish Congress, led by Samuel Bronfman and Saul Hayes. This took place late on a Friday, immediately after the Prime Minister had met with representatives of the Canadian Temperance Federation who had commended him for his unflagging commitment to temperance.[9] Why the meeting was scheduled at an hour when the Jewish community is busy preparing for the Sabbath, which arrives very early in the short days of February, is open to anyone's speculation. Did King actually hope no one would turn up because it interfered with religious practice? Or was it simply an expression of his cynicism? Or ignorance?

Whatever the Prime Minister's personal feelings about the issue, the meeting bore fruit. Two months later, on April 29, 1947 the Government of Canada renewed Privy Council Order 1647 of 1942 permitting five hundred child survivors of the Holocaust to enter Canada. This permission was given on condition that, for five years from the date of the orphan's arrival, "Canadian Jewish Congress unequivocally guarantees to the Minister of Mines and Resources of the Dominion of Canada full responsibility for the reception, placement and public charge liability for the project."[10] If the program proved successful, permission would be granted for an additional five hundred children at a later date. With the revived permission came the unmistakable message: to bring 1,000 young orphans into the country and to try to give them a new life might be noble, but also a considerable risk. Fred Blair had been blunt when he warned the government "the Jewish community will find it very difficult to look after their one thousand children satisfactorily."

This was not the first time the Jewish community had made such a pledge. In 1923 it had promised that if the Canadian government admitted 3,500 Rumanian Jews none of them would ever become a public charge. The Jewish community had lived up to this contract to the letter.

The requirement that Congress take full responsibility for the orphans was an onerous one. Like other western nations, Canada was fearful about permitting young survivors of the Holocaust to come into the country. Everyone feared that these children would have been

37

so damaged by their experiences that they could never be assimilated into normal life. And the Canadian public as well was quick to voice its misgivings about the troubles they would bring into the country.

Never before in Canadian history had a community assumed a responsibility of this nature; but never before in human history had the world faced the repercussions of mass murder on this scale. For Canadian Jewry, this Privy Council Order was not only the culmination of years of impassioned effort but also the beginning of the greatest undertaking in its history.

Few in number—40,000 families, spread over a vast country— Canadian Jews were aware that they had undertaken something that had never been done before. In their jubilation, they had no notion of the kind of difficulties that lay ahead. Many of the difficulties were those inherent in any child care project, large or small; others were owed to the scale of the job, and its geographic reach. Some, however, arose from particular conditions set by the Canadian government— or more precisely, governments, since the provinces carried much of the responsibility for child care under Canada's federal structure. We now turn to these conditions—the rules of the game.

CHAPTER THREE

The Rules of the Game

THE YOUNG ORPHANS who were permitted to settle in Canada were different from children who are orphaned by natural catastrophe. The latter know they are pitied, and that people want to help them, or at least feel they should help. In Nazi-occupied countries the psychological situation was exactly the opposite. The powers in that society were determined to destroy Jewish children, as they had already destroyed their parents; the children who survived did so only with help provided by others at great risk to themselves and their families. In Nazi territories young children understood that they would die unless they could control their tears, keep silent, and say good-bye to their families without protest. For others, to remember to substitute the name of a stranger for "Mama" became a matter of life and death.

When they arrived the youngsters knew little about Canada, and had no notion of the ways in which Canadian law protected them. Nor had the men and women who waited at Pier 21—or their counterparts who would wait at the railway stations in Montreal, Toronto, and Winnipeg—have given much thought to the subtleties of child welfare legislation. Preoccupied as they were with providing for the orphans' immediate needs, they spent little time analyzing why the Canadian government attached such demanding conditions to the granting of permission.

The departments of Immigration and Social Welfare insisted that the resettlement of the child survivors be carried out within the structure of the Canadian welfare system and in line with the newly-established principles of professional child welfare. In fact, the War Orphans Project of 1947-1949 was the first major child welfare program to be shaped by these new principles, and therefore was a test case. In a nutshell, Canadian Jewish Congress was to use the services of child welfare agencies to certify and supervise foster homes; adoption of children was the ultimate goal; and no children's institutions were to be part of the scheme.

The principles behind these rules had been developed during the late 1930s under the energetic leadership of Charlotte Whitton, director of the Canadian Council on Child Welfare (CCCW), a national federation of social agencies established to promote the development of child welfare programs across Canada. The new policies had provoked much controversy and opposition because they were seen as changing the face of Canadian child welfare; and they did, in two fundamental ways. First, they led to the removal of children from orphanages and other institutions, and their placement in individual foster homes. Second, trained professional social workers came to replace volunteer leadership in the community.

Whitton wanted to improve childcare by substituting foster homes for institutions and to develop a body of professional childcare workers who would put into practice the new psychological theories of child development and the dynamics of social groups. Only professional workers with training in understanding problems of family life, she argued, would have the skill to select the appropriate home placements and be able to avoid the disasters that had marked juvenile immigration in the past. She knew that it took more than a spontaneous burst of good will to provide long-term care for the children. The key to professional child placement, as preached by Whitton, was a careful match of child and home. Her credo was: "efficiency replaces spontaneity, system replaces sentiment, and method triumphs over muddle."[1]

A long-time child welfare activist, Whitton, as the director and driving force of the CCCW, had crusaded relentlessly for many years to raise standards of care for juvenile immigrants, and for neglected or dependent children. She helped define its policies and implement its programme; and under her vigorous leadership CCCW functions expanded beyond the original mandate to deal with children's problems to include the full spectrum of related social problems. Conseqently, the Council was seen to be the watchdog over all aspects of child and family life. When Whitton resigned in 1941, many could not imagine the Council having a future without its prime mover. This flamboyant and controversial woman was to leave her mark in Canadian history in more ways than one. She became mayor of Ottawa in 1951—Canada's first woman to hold that office.

However influential and sound Whitton's philosophy was in raising professional standards, it was not free of class and racial biases. She was an outspoken anti-semite who had played a significant role in preventing refugee children, Jewish as well as Armenian, from coming to Canada. Certainly not alone in holding these biases, Whitton's views on immigration reflected the Canadian version of "scientific" racism of the time. Essentially, this theory held that certain races possessed a monopoly of desirable characteristics; and that racial differences, being caused by heredity, were resistant to modification. In her public and private statements on immigration Whitton made little attempt to conceal these beliefs. For her, undesirable immigrants provided an explanation for Canada's social and economic problems—a curious paradox, since she herself believed in free will and individual merit. An even greater irony is the fact that her fervently pursued standards of child welfare found their first large-scale application with the Jewish children given visas under the War Orphans Project—a group she might have barred from coming to Canada. Given Whitton's influence, the application of the CCCW rules to the child survivors could scarcely have been free of anti-semitic prejudice.

In insisting that the War Orphans Project follow to the letter the new child welfare policies, the federal government was undoubtedly attempting to avoid the many abuses of past child immigration projects.

Beginning in the last century, Britain had often seen Canada as the solution for the alarming number of children who were begging in the streets and sleeping in gutters in east-end London. Dozens of individuals and organizations were involved in sending poor children to Canada. For the most part, the available historical evidence suggests that those who sent the children and those in Canada who oversaw their placement had high motives. They believed that life in the clean air of the new land, along with hard work and healthy discipline, would assure them of wholesome development. Often this was simply a naive dream with no understanding of the needs of a growing child and no awareness of the conditions in which they were placed.

The organizations concerned with child migration differed in quality, methods and philosophy—though, for the children, the end result was still exploitation and cheap labour. As few records were kept, it is hard to gauge how many were sent overseas during this philanthropic phase; but a report submitted by the Welfare Branch, Department of Health and Welfare, to the Interdepartmental Committee on Immigration in 1946 on the "Desirability of Child Immigration into Canada," estimates that 98,000 British children were brought to Canada from 1868 to 1943.[2]

The most famous of those involved in this movement was Thomas Barnardo, known as Doctor Bernardo even though he had never completed his medical studies. A would-be missionary driven by religious zeal Barnardo and his organization sent roughly 30,000 children across the Atlantic. Despite the high ideals of the organization, the reality was that "Dr. Barnardo's Children," as they became known in the press, were in essence little more than a source of farm labour for Canada.

Ranging in age from eight to sixteen, the children were taken first to receiving homes in various places in Ontario. Advertisements were then placed in local newspapers announcing the arrival of another "shipment of children" and inviting farmers to visit the home for a prospective "home boy or girl," not to be loved but to work. It was like saying a new load of produce had arrived for immediate delivery.

The child was rarely adopted; most were indentured. That meant, for example, a boy of ten years of age was signed over to a farmer for six years, until he was sixteen; for this he received his board, clothes, and at the end of the agreement $10.

As might be expected, there were a great many cases of physical and emotional abuse. Kenneth Bagnell, a trenchant critic of child migration gives one example of a child who had been placed in the care of an elderly woman in the Muskoka district and discovered to be attending school in the winter with no shoes. He was removed from her care and sent to another home near Port Perry, Ontario, where he fared little better, having to work from five in the morning until ten at night and being so poorly clad in winter that once, when he managed to go to school for a few weeks, he arrived with his feet almost frozen.[3]

From its early years the practice of sending children from Britain to Canada was the subject of investigation and controversy. By the 1920s, the British magazine *John Bull* featured articles headlined "Appalling Child Slavery" describing the cruelty with which some of the child migrants had been treated in Canada. But it wasn't until 1924 that a commission of four people was appointed in England and sent to Canada to obtain first-hand information about "the Canadian system for the placing and supervision of children brought to this Dominion from the United Kingdom." Headed by Margaret Bondfield, a member of the British parliament, the group landed in Montreal and began a ten-week journey to every province. Its report was another bland affair favouring child migration, but limiting it to children over the age of fourteen. It is testimony to the influence of market demand for cheap labour that the schemes continued as long as they did. Safeguards governing the welfare of child migrants sent out by British voluntary societies were not established until the Children Act of 1948 and even then were not put into practice until as late as the 1960s.[4]

In the early 1920s the Jewish community had a small-scale but rather more inspiring experience with settling European orphans. It began with the efforts of Dr. Elias Cheifitz, a Ukrainian Jew, who came to Canada from Europe in the summer of 1920 seeking homes for some of the thousands of destitute Jewish children in the Ukraine orphaned by the pogroms which followed the Communist revolution. He at first sought help in the United States, but none was forthcoming because of their immigration laws. Turning next to Canada he met a far more promising response. In no time Lyon Cohen, president of Canadian Jewish Congress, formed a committee to plan a country-wide organization under the leadership of Lillian Freiman, a prominent Ottawa figure in both Jewish and non-Jewish welfare work.[5]

The Department of Immigration and Colonization was then approached for permission to bring 1,000 children to Canada for adoption by Canadian families. Permission for 200 children was granted on the condition that arrangements by a reliable organization for their reception and adoption were made prior to their arrival.

A national conference described as "one of the most momentous gatherings of its kind held by Canadian Jewry" was held in Ottawa in October 1920 at the Chateau Laurier.[6] It led to the formation of an organization named the Jewish Women's Orphans Committee, and by the following month, Lillian Freiman, accompanied by Ida Seigler of Montreal, set off to visit all major cities between Halifax and Vancouver to talk about the orphans.

Men and women across the country responded with enormous enthusiasm. Thousands of people—Jewish and non-Jewish—participated in the campaign to raise money and collect large quantities of clothing. By the time Freiman and Seigler returned from their tour $96,000 had been raised, 43 huge cases of clothing collected, and local committees had formed. According to the written records, the level of enthusiasm for the project was explained by the fact that Canadian men and women had been told that no other country had brought orphans from the Ukraine to homes selected and waiting for them.

Considered in the context of the times the response was remarkable. Most Canadian Jews were themselves new arrivals and constantly bringing over relatives from "the old country." The large immigrant families, many struggling in the needle trades to make ends meet, nearly always opened their overcrowded homes to close relatives who had just come out of Eastern Europe. Under these conditions one would think very few families were in any position to offer homes to the Ukrainian orphans.

After arrangements on the home front were completed five men went to Europe in Febuary 1921 to select the children. The task of selecting children was said to have been "heartbreaking and difficult." They found that thousands wanted to go to Canada, but only a few were able to pass the physical and mental tests. In one week Dr. Joseph Leavitt examined 1,000 children and found only 46 whom he considered to be of "the standard required," and 8,000 to find 150 children. (Since most of the eligible children were older than six years, the age desired by most of the applicants, the number was reduced from 200 children to 150.) The children arrived in groups of five to seven from June to September in 1920. Most were adopted, some went to the U.S. to join their relatives, and a small number were placed in foster homes under the supervision of the committee.

Perhaps the best known figure in the story was Hirsch Hershman, who had accompanied Dr. Leavitt to the Ukraine. Almost single-handedly he found homes for over a hundred orphans brought to Montreal. This man with the neat beard, friendly eyes, and steel-rimmed eyeglasses hanging around his neck on a black ribbon would introduce himself with pride as "Hershman from *The Day*." He would add, "You may know me if you read the Yiddish newspapers."[7] (*Der Tag* was the most widely read Yiddish newspaper in Montreal.)

Originally from Bukovina, the energetic young anarchist was a typical activist of the Montreal Jewish immigrant society at the turn of the century. Ill-prepared as he and his fellows were to make their way in the New World, they felt a personal responsibility to shape their community along the lines of their humanitarian beliefs. Hershman is remembered by some for his ethical, humanitarian principles and ardent activism; by others for his love of books and learning. The first Jewish library in Montreal had its beginnings in his Hermione Street flat. Though it had only three rooms, one of them was set aside for books and visitors. More than anything else, however, Hershman is remembered for his role in finding homes for the war orphans.

On Fridays, after a long week selling newspapers, Hershman closed his stand at three o'clock, several hours earlier than usual. This gave him time before the Sabbath to parade the orphan children, a few at a time, along Esplanade Street, the centre of the Jewish community of the day, showing and praising them as a peddlar does his wares. A non-religious man himself, he presumably picked Fridays because that was when the neighbourhood streets were crowded with people preparing for the day of rest and prayer. It was also a time when he could most easily touch their hearts.

While the women hurried to the bakery to select the most perfectly braided challah in the pile of freshly baked breads, Hershman stood on the streets outside scrutinizing the passing faces, looking to match the orphans at his side with the right family. His successes have passed into Montreal Jewish folklore, as the following anecdote illustrates. It was told to me by David Rome.

One day, Hershman met Abe Cooperberg and persuaded him to take the bewildered, eight-year-old orphan named Yankel who stood holding tightly to his hand. The man from *The Day* assured Cooperberg that "he wouldn't regret it." Many years later, as an elderly man, Hershman was troubled by an eye condition and found himself referred to a young medical specialist named Dr. Cooperberg who recognized Hershman and did the exam free.

Hershman was impressed by the doctor's treatment and praised him to others with a fatherly pride. In telling his story Hershman never took credit for the pivotal role he had played in the young man's life and its successful outcome. Instead, with typical Jewish humour in talking about the chance encounter, Hershman highlighted his good luck in having saved the usual $25 fee for the consultation.

No matter where a child was settled Hershman tried to remain in touch with many of his orphans through letters and, at times, visits. They wrote him regularly keeping him informed about the care they were receiving from their guardians. If a problem arose between a child and foster parent, Hershman was often there to arbitrate, to guide, or scold as the situation required. And there were many such situations. In the words of Ben Lappin, "persons who were members of the Ukrainian orphan group revere the memory of this beloved man."[8]

Hershman also left a legacy of another kind. His adopted daughter, Faigie Hershman, originally an orphan from the Ukraine became an important figure in social work circles.[9] Faigie was responsible for setting up a foster home recruiting centre, an innovative concept for its time.

In general, however, child immigration schemes could not hold up to informed scrutiny. By the 1920s influential voices in Canada began questioning the practice and making proposals to restrict or end it. Charlotte Whitton condemned it as inhumane, while James Woodsworth, the respected MP and later first leader of the CCF, told the House of Commons: "We are bringing children into Canada in the guise of philanthropy, and turning them into cheap labourers."[10] It wasn't until 1940 that all provinces, except Saskatchewan and British Columbia, had reacted to public pressure by passing laws to bar child immigrants.

Despite these denunciations of unsupervised care and the resulting demise of the practice in the 1920s, many of the circumstances were repeated twenty years later when 6,000 British children were shipped to Canadian foster homes during the first two years of the Second World War. In 1939 as concern over the war grew in Britain, some 100,000 parents applied to have their children taken to safety abroad.

Canadian families were among the first to offer their homes and the newspapers in Britain were full of happy-looking children across the Atlantic.

At this stage only the better-off parents could afford to send their children overseas. They paid their children's passage themselves and also made arrangements about where their children should live. Many Britons thought it unfair that only wealthier children could be spirited to safety overseas, while children from poor families had to stay in Britain and endure the privation and dangers of war. The British government therefore set up a scheme to select a limited number of children from all classes to go overseas for the duration of the war.

By the summer of 1940 the British government formed the Children's Overseas Reception Boards (CORB) to send children from the less privileged homes to Canada. The government of MacKenzie King only agreed to this scheme if there would be strict quotas on who could come. It barred the thousands of German-Jewish children who had found refuge in Britain. (In the end a handful of Jewish children were included.)

As it turned out, only 6,000 children arrived. Another 14,000 were awaiting their turn to come to Canada when the plan came to an abrupt end with the September 1940 sinking of the liner *City of Benares* and the deaths of the hundreds of children aboard. The tragedy convinced authorities that the Atlantic had become too dangerous and the scheme was dropped.

For the children who reached Canada, however, child care in 1940 was a haphazard affair, despite planning conferences and much talk of professional standards. Many provinces lacked the organization and the staff for supervised foster care, and serious problems arose. In the early days child placement workers began to worry that many people were offering to take a child "to help the war effort," or because it was the humane and patriotic thing to do, and disregarded the extent of the responsibilities they were undertaking.

This then was the background which faced the Jewish War Orphans

Project. The new child welfare principles, although not yet implemented with any consistency, were well-conceived and in time would prove sound for Canadian children under public care. Unfortunately, when applied to the young Holocaust orphans and the men and women accepting responsibility for their care, the strict application of these principles created a number of practical problems. Chief among them was the requirement that Congress assign the care of the children to professional personnel from accredited child care agencies. In principle this was appropriate, for it meant that foster homes had to meet standards set by Children's Aid Societies and that homes would be supervised by professional staff.

In practice, it was unworkable. The established agencies simply did not have the adequate staff and resources for the new task. Nor did they have the psychological insights and exceptional powers of understanding needed for those very special young people. Perhaps no one had. Complicating matters was the fact that the years 1947 to 1949 brought to Canada not only the 1,123 child survivors, but also roughly 15,000 Jewish refugees requiring varying kinds of care and support. Resources were stretched to the limit. Asked to evaluate the refugee services provided by Congress in October, 1949 Mary Palevsky, deputy executive director of the New York Association of New Americans, reported that "there has been general agreement among the officers of Congress that they had not foreseen the magnitude of the task which they had undertaken when they had assumed overall responsibility for receiving and settling thousands of immigrants in the short time allotted to them."[11]

In great part this was due to the uncertain and unpredictable nature of the program itself. DP immigration did not stem from a specific national legislative act, but as a series of special labour projects sponsored in varying combinations by government, industry and voluntary groups, and authorized by specific orders-in-council. As a result, Congress never knew from one project to another whether its advocacy with government would succeed, or if successful, how much time would be available for implementation. For the immigrants sponsored by the fur and clothing industry the Congress was responsible for meeting the arrivals in Halifax, paying for inland transportation, and providing housing. It was never clarified whose responsibility it was if the immigrant became ill, unemployed or pregnant. As it turned out, Jewish Family Welfare had to provide the financial and emotional support for people in that category.

Added to the pressure of a community already heavily burdened were the financial conditions attached to the Government's permission for the War Orphans Project. All costs for the orphans—ocean passage, housing, food, clothing, education, medical and social services—were to be assumed by the Jewish community. Fortunately, major international organizations (the International Refugee Organization and the Jewish Immigration Aid Society) had agreed to pay the overseas transportation for each youth. Generous as this contribution was, it nevertheless constituted only a minor portion of the costs which would have to be borne by the Jewish community the moment the newcomers disembarked in Halifax. Despite the fabled fortunes of well-known families like the Bronfmans, the funds were to come largely from the personal donations of people who were of modest means.

The Canadian government had made clear to all segments of the country that it would consider *only* applications for groups of refugee children by "permanent, responsible organizations, financially sound and with facilities." The one organization other than Congress to submit a concrete proposal which met all the requirements was the Catholic Immigrant Aid Society. However, that project was never implemented. Among the organizations which had carried the bulk of British juvenile immigration before the war, the Fairbridge Farm School of Duncan, B.C. was the only one to respond to the government offer and it brought twenty-eight British children into the country in 1947.

The underlying reason for framing eligibilty in this way was obvious. In its reluctance to admit young Jewish orphans into the country the

Canadian government had made no secret of its dismal view of their future prospects, and did everything possible to shield itself from unforeseeable demands. The clear message—don't expect to be bailed out when there is trouble—was unmistakable.

Fortunately, although the Order-in-Council stipulated that the Jewish community would assume all financial responsibilities, Canada proved more generous in that all three levels of government—municipal, provincial, and federal—paid for many services required when the occasion demanded. For instance, Congress was never billed for any hospitalization or other institutional care. The manner in which this is recorded in Congress files suggests that it was interpreted as a voluntary act of generosity to the Jewish community, and very much appreciated by an agency swamped by overwhelming demands.

But this was in the future. In the interim between the granting of permission and the arrival of the young refugees, the only thing that could be confidently predicted was that the War Orphans Project would depend upon the massive contribution of volunteers. Unfortunately, responsibilities between the professionals and volunteers were never adequately clarified—and perhaps could not have been. Unresolved antagonisms would plague the Project and squander valuable energy throughout its duration.

The result was an irreconcilable conflict between the volunteers who were in every way indispensable to the Project and the professional agencies, especially in the large cities of Montreal and Toronto. For example, emotional appeals called upon people of good will to act like family. When they came forward however, they were treated impersonally as "clients," and brusquely screened and evaluated by newly trained "professional social workers"—the graduates of a young, still-to-be-tested profession. Instead of being recognized for their altruism, even men and women who were acknowledged pillars of society were told they must be examined for the suitability of their homes or the wholesomeness of their marital and family life. It is understandable that many kind-hearted people became resentful and refused to submit to routine evaluation. In consequence, according to Mrs. Toni Robinson who had played a leading role in recruiting volunteers and finding resources to help the youngsters, "a goodly number of homes were lost."

Some of the problems arose from the administrative structures of the agencies themselves. In Montreal, for example, the Family and Child Welfare Department of the Baron de Hirsch Institute accepted the heavy burden of caring for the orphans at a time when it was facing numerous problems clamouring for solution. Founded in 1890 with a large contribution from the English statesman-philanthropist Baron Moses de Hirsch to deal with the problems of new immigrants, it grew into an organization capable of handling virtually all the welfare and relief work of the Jewish community. Despite its long history it had not succeeded in achieving stability and lacked community support. Part of the problem was its odd structure in which two separate departments for family and child care were administered by one executive but reported to two separate and competing boards. Just as serious, its staff, which had been evaluated by external examiner Mary Palevsky in 1949, was described as "unqualified and subject to excessive turnover." To make matters even worse, in July 1947 its executive director, David Weiss, had only just arrived from New York and had had no opportunity to plan for the wide range of activities required for the refugee programme.

In Toronto the Jewish Family and Child Services, the main agency, like its Montreal counterpart, suffered from chronic problems of understaffing and high turnover. However, its difficulties were considerably offset by the stability and continuity of its board and executive.

Whatever their location in the country, all of the Jewish welfare agencies involved in the Project were plagued by the structure set in place by Congress. The directors of Congress understood that the needs of these young people went beyond what most agencies could be expected to provide, so in order to enlarge available resources they set up a Co-ordinating Committee to oversee the Project. No one could foresee the difficulties this was to cause. The Committee consisted of laypersons of widely differing orientations—what appeared to unite them was the belief that social workers were an unnecessary evil.[12] For his part David Weiss complained to the board of Congress that "the Jewish community in Montreal does not accept the role and leadership of the professional social worker."[13]

The conflicts between volunteers and professionals took other forms as well. In Montreal the reception centre where the youngsters were placed upon arrival soon became the target of such community enthusiasm that it was impossible to keep it under control. Well-meaning people took the children for sight-seeing tours and visits to wealthy homes; they lavished gifts and expensive clothing upon some, and exposed others to ill-advised publicity stunts involving speeches and photographers, and in general created a highly-charged emotional atmosphere in which it was difficult for the social workers to do their jobs.[14] The excitement was unsettling for these bewildered adolescents. When in due course, community enthusiasm waned, and the time came for Cinderella to leave the ball and settle down to the humdrum existence of furnished rooms, menial jobs, and relief budgets, it was the social workers who bore the brunt of the youngsters' disenchantment.[15]

Another controversy which arose time and time again, particularly in the larger cities, revolved around the issue of free versus paid foster homes. Good foster homes are never plentiful anywhere, but at the time an acute post-war housing shortage aggravated by the competing needs of hundreds of immigrants combined to make home-finding a vexing problem. Community leaders favoured free homes, the professionals paid ones. As some volunteers saw it, good people who truly cared about the orphans would not expect payment for their parenting. Monetary payment somehow, in their view, diminished the depth of commitment, and tainted the sincerity of people welcoming the young survivors into their homes as family members. On the other hand, social workers knew from experience how difficult it was to find good foster homes at any time. As well, the professionals reasoned that paying for a home gave them some control over what went on in it. Dora Wilensky, the director of Toronto's Jewish Family and Child Welfare, stated her views firmly to Congress Headquarters in October 1948 when she said, "a good paying home with middle-class people give the best opportunity for adjustment and satisfaction."[16]

Inherent in this debate was the troublesome question of how much to pay for a good home. At the time, the going foster home rates in Montreal and Toronto were $40 a month for children up to sixteen, and $50 for youth over sixteen. As the supply of available homes remained far below the number needed, the question of whether more money would produce a better supply of homes became yet another contested issue.

But long before such matters became a problem many obstacles had first to be overcome and complicated plans formulated before the Project could become a reality.

CHAPTER FOUR

Gearing Up in Canada

PERMISSION GRANTED AT LAST, men and women in all walks of life across the country began immediately to prepare for the arrival of the orphans. And often they had stars in their eyes: many pictured the "orphans" for whom they were planning as frail little girls who would blossom with the loving care they would lavish on them. Although they were given some tangible details to focus on, including the numbers to be allowed in the country and projected dates of arrival, there was little substantive information to direct them. All they had were the emotional memoranda sent out from Congress headquarters in Montreal stressing the desperate need for homes: "If there is room in your heart, there is room in your home for a Jewish war orphan."

Congress was as confounded as the most remote Canadian community. The European situation was unstable and changed from day to day so that well-defined policies frequently had to give way to last minute changes based on sparse details received from overseas. A typical letter written on December 5, 1947 by Manfred Saalheimer from Europe, where he was sent by Congress to select the youngsters and expedite their passage, gives a sense of the conditions under which everyone worked:

> Giving advance information on children's transports involves a certain amount of crystal [ball] gazing. Due to the rapid succession in which we are able to take the children out of Europe, it is usually just about at the last day before the

transport leaves the embarkation centre that the composition of the transport is finalized.[1]

And then there was "The General Plan" which was less a plan than a more detailed reiteration of the conditions to the permission granted. First, as well as assuming all financial costs, Congress was to be the sole agency dealing with federal, provincial and municipal authorities. Second, while adoption of the children was to be the ultimate goal, certification of foster homes as well as the ongoing supervision of the children in those homes was to be carried out by social welfare agencies. Institutionalizing childen, except in the earliest stages of their arrival in temporary receiving centres, was not permitted. Finally, in order to centralize all activities and draw on all possible community resources, Congress elected to set up a co-ordinating committee nationally and in areas where children were to be placed.

What at the outset seemed like a single, straightforward guide expanded in a short time into hundreds of very complex formulas. And with assembly line regularity all manner of problems originating from across the country and abroad were sent to Montreal for solutions. Individuals and agencies read their own meanings based on their own experiences and expectations into the memos. For example, Winnipeg did not follow, as it was meant to, the example of Montreal and Toronto in opening a reception centre. Originally the vacant local orphanage was to be converted into a temporary residence; instead it was decided that the children would be settled in permanent homes the very day they arrived.

The confusion was almost predictable. Canadian Jews had to re-orient themselves to having decisions made by a central body, Congress. They had grown accustomed, because of the terms of Canadian immigration legislation, to acting as individual sponsors of refugees. Under the terms of permission granted for the orphans it was Congress who made the rules.

The black and white photograph of the planning session at Congress headquarters at 1121 St. Catherine Street West in Montreal could have been modelled on hundreds of historical paintings, especially the Dutch masters, which hang in art museums around the world. The picture had no title, but if it had, it would have read, "The Canadian Fathers of the War Orphans Project." It shows a group of dignified burghers, roughly of the same age, dressed in dark suits and wearing grave expressions. Together, as reported in the recorded minutes of these meetings, they attempted to define the boundaries, always in flux, of the area within which they must operate—somewhere between the limitless boundaries of an ideal world and the actual borders of human energy and generosity. As leaders of their community they had to learn how to estimate the resources of their community, how to mine them, and perhaps hardest of all, how to multiply them.

At the head of the table sat a tall, distinguished, white-haired man with a commanding presence. He spoke forcefully and pointedly, having long since learned how to hold an audience's attention and attract people to his causes. The post of command had fallen naturally and without contest to Benjamin Robinson. Appointed Justice of the Superior Court of Quebec years later in 1960, he became the second Canadian Jew to hold high office in the province's courts. He was one of the first to both articulate a vision of bringing child survivors to Canada and to summon others to help him devise a plan for its realization. Whether his experience in the courts of law had endowed him with the wide-angled view demanded by the project he spear-headed remained to be tested. But perhaps it was his family background that most influenced the qualities of his leadership.

Born in Russia in 1892 Robinson grew up in Portland, Maine in a religious family steeped in Jewish history and culture. When asked, he attributed his interest in the plight of immigrants to his parents "who seemed to devote endless days to helping their oppressed relatives and friends migrate from Russia. Our home was a virtual immigrant aid society and impressed me greatly."[2]

A graduate of McGill Law School in 1918, after establishing himself in practice Robinson became interested in helping with the reception and settlement of Jewish immigrants who were then arriving in considerable numbers from Europe. That experience served him well when he took on the leadership for devising a plan and receiving a first group of 140 youngsters in a short period of sixteen weeks. It was one thing to figure out the logistics which allowed few options, it was quite another to know what constituted good parenting for unknown youngsters of differing ages, backgrounds, and fractured childhoods. The essence of good communal parenting had to be defined in a way never before thought about; as well as an understanding of what one could realistically expect from parents already saddled with their own family obligations.

Many of these men laying the cornerstones for the Project served as chairmen of various important sub-comittees—home-finding, employment, education, hospitality, clothing, and finance. As builders and captains of successful businesses and industries they were confident and able to draw on many organizational skills. Accustomed to overcoming obstacles and "getting things done," they naively believed that the project could be completed in three months.

Whatever direction planning took, it rested on two clearly articulated principles: the promotion of independence and self-sufficiency, and the assumption that every youth was capable of determining his own life. There may have been no alternative to giving the highest priority to the promotion of independence given the strain on resources; but in another sense it was meant to convey a message of great significance. It indicated to each youngster that he or she was considered healthy and potentially capable of determining their own life.

But before the project could get off the ground at all, one crucial stumbling block had to be overcome—Canada's federal structure. Congress had to gain the permission of the nine provincial governments (Newfoundland had not yet joined Confederation). Under the B.N.A.

Act immigration was the joint responsibility of the federal and provincial governments. In practice, however, at the time of the War Orphans Act the provinces left immigration largely to the federal government. Nevertheless, Section 92 of the British North America Act (Property and Civil Rights) made it necessary to comply with the rules and regulations of the various provincial Child Welfare Acts before one orphan could be brought to Canada.

This was not easily done. By 1940 all provinces except Saskatchewan and British Columbia had passed laws to stop child immigration because of the mishandling of juvenile immigrants in the past. Also, the country's provincial deputy ministers responsible for welfare were unanimous in their concerns about the impact of large numbers of immigrant children on an already acute shortage of foster homes for Canadian children.[3]

Despite talk of professional standards, child welfare practice in Canada in the second part of the 1940s was a haphazard affair with many agencies advancing at different speeds—and some not advancing at all. Child welfare services had developed in widely different ways and speeds in the various provinces.[4] Regional disparities in both rhetoric and practice were legion, with many provinces lacking the organization and staff for supervised foster care. In all provinces, except among the Catholic majority in Quebec, the Children's Aid Societies carried the responsibility for child care. (The Protestant community in Quebec developed its own CAS). Formed by groups of citizens who applied to their provincial government for recognition, the CAS's were largely volunteer organizations employing a small professional staff which ran shelters for children. Although some provinces had well-established and competently run services for children, even the best lacked the staff they needed.

Ontario, the first province to develop CAS's, and the first to appoint a provincial superintendent for neglected children, was considered the leader in the field. In contrast, Alberta's penny-pinching services did not meet Canadian Council of Child Welfare (CCCW) standards and during the 1940s were subjected to a series of investigations. A Commission of Inquiry in the summer of 1947 concluded that Alberta had made little progress in professionalizing its child care services. New Brunswick's performance was also repeatedly castigated by the CCCW and seen as impervious to the recomendations of child welfare experts. In Nova Scotia, as well, the CAS's were poorly financed, understaffed and struggling against heavy odds to provide a minimum of security for the children affected.

As in so many other fields, Quebec was a special case. The Deputy Minister of Health, Dr. Jean Grégoire, supervised a confusion of child care agencies affiliated for the most part with religious organizations and governed by the Quebec Charities Act. As Congress contemplated the task of negotiating with Quebec, it could not have done so without trepidation. Fresh in everyone's mind was the memory of 1944 when the St-Jean Baptiste Society, supported by many Montreal city councillors, organized a petition of 100,000 signatures requesting that the government ban the entry of Jewish immigrants.

There was only one way to get full provincial permission. Somebody had to travel from one end of the country to the other, stopping in each provincial capital along the way. The assignment fell automatically to Saul Hayes, the Executive Director of Congress. Hayes' talents as an astute leader had already been demonstrated. Sam Bronfman, who was known for his ability to see things long before anybody else, had been the first to notice this tall, reserved young lawyer, and had appointed him as director of the United Jewish Relief Agencies in 1938.

There wasn't a person better suited for the task. Hayes, a native Montrealer, was a member of an old Canadian Jewish family which had imbued him with a profound sense of community service. After graduating in law from McGill University in 1932, he lectured at the Montreal School of Social Work before joining a law firm. When the Canadian Jewish Congress was re-established in 1934 Hayes became an active volunteer in its Youth Committee as well as its Bureau of

Saul Hayes at his desk at the Canadian Jewish Congress
office, Montreal, mid 1940s.
Canadian Jewish Congress National Archives

Social and Economic Research.

This was an important year for the Bureau. Louis Rosenberg, who for some time had been gathering data for the first comprehensive study of Canada's Jews, was in the final stages of completing his work, so Hayes was in a position to contribute to the project. Published in 1940 as *Canada's Jews: A Social and Economic Study of the Jews in Canada,* and re-published in 1993 by McGill-Queen's University Press, it is an outstanding socio-demographic study of a particular Canadian ethnic or religious group. The knowledge and insights about Canada's Jews which Hayes would have acquired from that experience, coupled with his legal training, gave him just the solid background he would need to meet the challenges of the turbulent days that lay ahead on both the domestic and international fronts.

Hayes left his law practice with little ambivalence. His longtime colleague, David Rome understood that "in his heart, Hayes was not very enthusiastic about practising law and really dreamed about becoming an academic, a career then closed to Jews." When asked by Bronfman in 1938 to work for the Jewish Refugee Committee, later re-named the United Jewish Refugee and War Relief Agencies, which was formed to rescue and resettle Jewish victims of Hitler's persecution, Hayes found his true calling. Two years later he was appointed executive director and in 1942 his position expanded to include the executive directorship of Canadian Jewish Congress, a position which he held until his retirement in 1974.

Among Hayes' many roles in serving refugees and the Jewish community there is one in particular which dominates. In 1944, when the United Nations Relief and Rehabilitation Agency's second meeting was held in Montreal, Hayes was instrumental in bringing together the various representatives of Jewish groups from around the world, all of whom wished to be heard by UNRRA. Their most pressing issue was to rescind the ruling, passed at UNRRA's first meeting, of excluding from UNRRA benefits "enemy aliens" or the "stateless"— two categories which included thousands of Jewish victims of Nazism.

Up until then all efforts had failed. UNRRA was finally persuaded to hear one representative. Hayes' effective diplomacy had already earned him wide respect, and he was chosen as spokesperson for world Jewry at the Second Session of UNRRA which was convened at the Windsor Hotel in Montreal on September 16, 1944. This was the first time since Versailles that an international organization representing world powers allowed Jewish representation. Hayes petitioned the Council to recognize any Jewish national of enemy countries or a stateless person as having the same rights as members of nationalities recognized by the United Nations. The petitition, of enormous significance for Jewish refugees, was accepted and reversed the earlier refusal.

Thereafter, Congress worked in close cooperation with UNRRA and Hayes, as Executive Director, sat on the international executive of many of its auxiliary voluntary agencies. In 1945 he represented Canadian Jewish Congress in San Francisco at the founding assembly of the United Nations. And a year later, he was invited to Paris to attend the signing of the Allied peace treaties with Hungary and Italy.

Perhaps it was a touch of exaggeration, but also a mark of affection, that Hayes, as Rome put it, was called by his admirers "Our Jewish Prime Minister." Vincent Massey, a former Governor General of Canada, addressing a Plenary session of Congress, described Saul Hayes as one of the most outstanding public servants Canada had produced. Yaacov Herzog, formerly Israel's Ambassador to Canada, said that Hayes was the most distinguished Jewish public servant in the diaspora.

David Rome also believed that Saul Hayes personified and became a model for the new professional Jewish civil servant. And as the journalist, J.B. Salsberg, wrote in a memorial tribute in the *Canadian Jewish News* in February 1980, "that was exactly what was needed at the time to handle the new and very complex situations." Hayes' respect for authority and adherence to the letter of the law set a new course for dealing with government. Rather than regarding the law as a nuisance to be circumvented, which was how the community had approached government policy, his keen understanding of how government worked led him to utilize the law fully and constructively.

Ethel Bassin, a woman active in the community life of Regina, remembers Hayes as an impressive figure who projected an air of mastery and savoir-faire.

> He was tall and handsome with a fine head of hair and a trimmed moustache. He had all the attractiveness of 'The Arrow Man' in collar advertisements, and we held him in high esteem as Bronfman's right hand and speech writer. We felt that we were in the presence of an intelligent, superior person, although he was never uppity, but always gracious and interesting to talk to.

Quebec, home of Congress' National Office, was logically the first province on Hayes' agenda. Besides, as he wrote in his memoirs, "I started in Quebec because we don't have as much red tape as we do in every other province."[5] But how does one go about obtaining permission from a department of Social Welfare when in fact one doesn't exist? It was the Church, although it held an ill-defined connection with the department of Health, which held exclusive authority over this field in place of a department of Social Welfare. There was no one with whom to discuss the matter. Despite this executive vacuum the jurisdiction was still a provincial one and it was necessary to receive approval for the project from *someone*.

Hayes tried many times to contact the Premier of Quebec, Maurice Duplessis. But Duplessis rarely gave interviews and rarely answered requests. This was well known and did not apply only to requests from the Jewish community. Even approaches from the Canadian National Committee on Refugees in support of Congress' project were ignored, despite or because of the fact that its board consisted of prominent people from the Anglophone community. (One was Cairine Wilson, the first woman appointed to the Canadian Senate and in 1949 the first Canadian woman delegate to the United Nations.) This presented a dilemma—either break the law or forget about obtaining provincial approval. Both alternatives were unthinkable.

The novel strategy which the Jewish community had developed over the years in dealing with government was not working in this case. Out of necessity an informal approach known as the "porte-parole" (mouthpiece) was how matters of concern to the Jewish community were handled. Either Morris Pollock, a Quebec businessman, or the Montreal lawyers, Joe Cohen and Leon Cristohl, would arrange to have dinner with Duplessis whenever an issue arose which fell under provincial jurisdiction. The same strategy was also used in Montreal with mayor Camillien Houde when the issue was a municipal one.

Since Hayes was not able to arrange an appointment with any provincial minister, he sent a long letter to Duplessis outlining the plan in detail—the number of children to be brought into Quebec, the number of homes sought, the process of selection of suitable homes, the motivation of prospective foster parents, and as much of the children's backgrounds as was known. No reply was received. Hayes then sent a letter indicating that if he did not receive any further correspondence on the matter he would conclude that the plan as presented was accepted and that he could proceed. A copy of the letter was sent to the minister closest to the area of social services. After a thirty day delay, a letter was received stating that Quebec had no objections.

Following this first victory Hayes boarded a train heading west. Travelling alone, he would eventually visit every province except Prince Edward Island (which had only one known Jewish person living there) and every Department of Social Welfare, or the minister in charge of Child Welfare if there was no such department.

Sometimes Hayes' task proved astonishingly simple. In Saskatchewan there was no specific ministry for Child Welfare. It was the Minister of Roads and Transportation, the Honorable John Taylor Douglas, MLA for Rosetown, a regional transportation centre, who had responsibility for carrying out the Child Welfare Act. Hayes requested an interview, and was told that the Minister was staying at Regina's Hotel Saskatchewan, the elegant, well-appointed CPR hotel where all major social and political events were held. An appointment was made to meet the minister in his hotel room. When Hayes arrived for his appointment, he "was greeted by a gentleman wearing a rumpled pair of pants held up by thick suspenders, an open shirt and felt slippers."[6] As soon as Hayes presented the request the Minister quickly admitted that he knew a great deal more about the sorry state of roads in the farming areas of Saskatchewan than he did about the Child Welfare Act. Still, he was interested and co-operative and readily gave his approval.

The other provincial governments proved tougher. Although they had been unfailingly sympathetic to Congress' plans when first approached by letter and had given their approval in principle, the additional demands made by some when plans were about to turn into action, showed their hesitation.

In Manitoba, the Minister of Public Health and Welfare, the Honourable Ivan Schultz, insisted that a survey be undertaken to ascertain the number of satisfactory foster homes available in Winnipeg for the children.[7] These demands were not unreasonable in checking for general conditions such as cleanliness or family composition, but quite unrealistic when attempting to make a good fit of temperament and culture between a child and a family. How was a prospective home to be evaluated for these qualities when the child to be placed was still in Europe? Clearly, the carefully supervised adoption and foster care procedures developed with respect to Canadian children could not be applied to this European group. In the end the Minister listened to reason and dropped his demand.

Alberta, through its Minister of Public Health and Welfare, the Hon. W.W. Cross, expressed its uneasiness about possible future burdens that might fall on its domain. It extracted from Congress eight detailed categories of guarantee, to reinforce the ones the federal government had already imposed. The following four have been selected to illustrate

Alberta's concern that no loophole or ambiguous interpretaton of their permission be left to the vagaries of this potentially troublesome project; and its reluctance to contribute anything other than permission.

1. Every child brought into the Province under this scheme will be given a thorough physical and mental examination at the time of selection of the child, and a medical certificate showing that the child is free from disease and in sound mental and physical condition shall be sent to the Child Welfare Commission prior to the admission of the child into the Province.

2. The Society undertakes and agrees to assume full responsibility for the maintenance and necessary medical attention of each child brought into the Province until he or she reaches twenty-one years.

3. The Society be responsible for providing proper educational facilities in accordance with all the requirements of the Department of Education.

4. The Society undertakes and agrees to provide a bond in a form satisfactory to the Minister in such sum as will represent an amount equal to the number of children to be brought into the Province.[8]

Nonetheless, a combination of Hayes' rhetorical and persuasive skills and a generalized compassionate reaction to the young survivors worked in the Project's favour. In a short time all the provinces had given their consent, including the approval by default from Quebec.

With the *sine qua non* requirement of provincial permission fulfilled, the necessary next step was the formation of a nationwide programme consistent with the structure of the Canadian welfare system. Congress began by developing a network of committees, composed of representatives of major community groups, within a pyramid structure which stretched from the national planning committee in Montreal to every Jewish community in the country having ten or more resident Jewish families. This proved too unwieldy and before the youngsters arrived was changed to communities of at least 80 Jewish families in order to provide adequate supervision. Translated into numbers, Canada divided into 85 Jewish communities: 38 in Ontario, 29 in Western Canada, and 18 in Quebec and the Maritimes. According to this formula 416 children would go to Ontario, 390 to Quebec, 111 to Manitoba, 23 Saskatchewan, 22 to Alberta, 19 to the Maritimes and 19 to British Columbia.

Virtually every Jewish organization in the country was mobilized. In Montreal alone, for example, the Sponsor and Housing Committee of Congress had representation from the following: five chapters of B'nai Brith, the Brigadier Kisch Branch of Canadian Legion, Ezrah Ladies Society, Hadassah, Jewish Child and Family Welfare Bureau, Jewish Immigrant Aid Society, Jewish Junior Welfare League, Knights of Pythias, The Maccabees Modin Hive, Malbish Arumim Society, National Council of Jewish Women, Organization for Rehabilitation and Training, parent-teacher associations and young member groups of synagogue and parochial schools, and the YMHA.

In smaller centres there were fewer organizations, but the will to help was just as powerful. The above-quoted Ethel Bassin described the organizing in Regina this way:

> The men organized, the women carried things out. In Regina we were a community of about two hundred families and everyone without exception was involved. We were a tight, cohesive community. My husband Eddy was a chartered accountant and a community leader. He was involved in simply everything, so therefore I was too, and we had an open house with all kinds of social activities going on all the time. Boy

was it a busy place! And I loved it.

During the war we knitted constantly for the soldiers and war relief, and collected tin foil for the Red Cross. It was a very emotional time, and all we could think of was 'what can we do?' After hearing about the horrors, to think that children were coming, was like welcoming family. Those people who weren't in a position to take an orphan for whatever reason, found other ways to contribute. Most of the men owned retail stores so they made sure the youth had all their clothing and material needs satisfied. And one thing for sure, Rose Hoffer could always be counted on for a steady supply of shoes. I don't know why, but she had a special liking for them, and always had lots to give away.

Anyway, those kids who arrived in Regina were taken care of by everybody—it was a total community effort given in a quiet way, nurturing the good. And to think of it in the light of today, it is rather remarkable how natural it was for all of us to make allowances for individual differences. I tell you we seemed to spend all our time time attending meetings, or doing whatever was needed by those kids.

In those years, life in Canada revolved around the immediate and extended family, and social life in community organizations. Aware of the multitude of productive service groups throughout the country, it was with understandable confidence that the leaders of Congress accepted the government contract.

It was with absolute conviction in the power of family life to restore the traumatized youth to health that they sent out solicitations for homes. No one could know how difficult it was going to be to find those homes; and no one could predict the social and emotional problems rooted in the hopes and fears, dreams and misconceptions, always unique, of each "resettlement case." Offers of free homes flooded the regional and national offices when the Project was first publicized, but these offers were chiefly for very young children. When it was learned that the group would consist of older youngsters many families were ready to accept girls, but girls were only roughly one-third of the group.

Also, time and experience would later prove that being taken into a family was no guarantee of happiness; and that enthusiastic volunteers were not necessarily the best suited to be foster parents, either by circumstance or temperament.

Appeals for homes were first circulated by word of mouth at all service group meetings, and followed by a full-page article in the Congress Bulletin.

WILL YOU OPEN YOUR HOME?

Will you take into your home one of the war orphans whom the Canadian Jewish Congress has brought to Canada? Your home is urgently needed if Congress is to continue this, its greatest undertaking in the history of Canadian Jewry.

Will you undertake to find a home for one of these young people and help to pay for it until the young man or woman is established?

If you say yes, the Congress will be able to bring one more Jew from Europe. If your answer is no, a Jewish orphan who might have come to Canada will be forced to remain in Europe.

What is wanted from you is basically a place where this young man or woman can sleep and eat and where he can have a measure of home life where he can bring the friends he may make and where he can become a companion to you and to your sons and daughters. He will appreciate your friendship and your love. The most experienced social workers in Canada will continue to help your new friend and will deal with all problems that will arise.

You are not being asked to enter into any legal arrangements.

Just take him into your home. Introduce him to your friends, let him share your life, let him share your home as it is.

These young people (their ages run mostly from 14 to 18) are cheerful, friendly, cultured, experienced and youthful. They are on the threshold of a new life here. They are prepared to go to work and to learn Canada by living Canadian lives.

This is a great opportunity for you and a great challenge.

If you are not Canadian-born yourself, you will remember how you felt when you first came to this country, how badly you wanted friends and a home. You are now in a position to do as much for a young Jewish man or woman who is starting life anew in this country.

It became evident very quickly that this approach would not produce the numbers of homes needed and something else was required. A letter written during a sleepless night by hand "because it was too early in the morning, or too late at night to use a typewriter" by Hayes on October 19, 1948 to Benjamin Robinson, Chairman of the Project, has an unmistakable tone of panic.

A scare must be thrown into the Jewish community at once. The whole of the Canadian Jewish community must be apprised of the crisis that if homes are not offered we must go back to Europe to cancel many of the plans and go back to Ottawa and confess our inability to absorb 1,000 or even several hundred war orphans.

Hayes then recommends, based on his consultation with other members of the community, the necessary steps that must be undertaken:

A special four-page bulletin to go out to 2700 subscribers solely devoted to the crisis; a special pithy scarefying [sic] letter to the residents of our bigger communities; a mass meeting in every large community to which a recent arrival from Europe will be one of the speakers, preceded by a campaign in the Yiddish-Anglo-Jewish press.

The letter ends with: "Scare, Scare, Scare ! Crisis, Crisis, Crisis ! Cessation, Cessation, Cessation. This campaign may well produce a few hundred homes."

In spite of what was done, there was still an insuffcient number of offers for homes. The urgency to find homes never slackened and produced a state of continuous crisis. The leaders had been let down by the community. A year later in May 1948 the appeal that was sent out to all communities by Congress used equally strong, desperate language: "FROM SHMAD... (shame in Yiddish) FROM SHAME...FROM SHAMBLES...DELIVER THEM... Open your heart—Open your home to a Jewish war orphan!"

Vigorous home-finding campaigns were invariably based on guilt. Families were constantly reminded by letter, through the press, and over the radio that after watching helplessly the annihilation of European Jewry they now had the privilege of helping a war orphan to secure a new start in life. And implicit in the publicity was the warning that indifference was tantamount to the evasion of a traditional Jewish responsibility originating in Exodus 22: "Thou shalt not afflict a widow or fatherless child. If thou afflict them in any wise and they cry at all unto me I will surely hear their cry."

And then a few months later Congress sent out a ten-page booklet entitled "If There's Room in Your Home, There's Room in Your Heart" ending with a personal letter signed by Saul Hayes. This time a somewhat different approach was used. In addition to the highly-charged emotional words of appeal, short biographies of some the children were included addressing what Congress had come to recognize as

A desperate appeal to the Jewish community that
appeared in the *Congress Bulletin*, May 1948.
Canadian Jewish Congress National Archives

the source of people's fears and hesitations to accept an orphan in their homes. "Michael is seventeen... his father was a doctor, his mother an accomplished pianist. After two years in a Polish ghetto his parents smuggled him into hiding with the help of friendly peasants. Michael's past is ashes; but his future is bright... if you will help him. He wants to work his way through, to study medicine. Will you give him the new start his courage so richly deserves?"

The same booklet printed heartening letters—either authentic or simulated— from Canadian foster parents to their friends:

I'm so pleased with myself that I must drop you a line and pass along the formula for the most wonderful feeling I've had in years ...We've added a new member to our family.

You've heard that Congress is bringing a thousand war orphans across from Europe. These kids lost their parents during the war, and the only homes they've known for years have been cellars, DP camps and the like...

Well we held a little family council, and decided that the very least we could do was to give one of these youngsters a home. It gave me a genuine thrill to see how our own kids fell in with the idea, and we're all very happy with Arthur.

He's seventeen, a good head taller than me, highly intelligent, handy with tools (he's got our radio actually working on short wave!)—and you should hear him sing! What amazes me most is how these children kept their heads, their sense of humour, their cheerfulness through all the difficulties undergone. One of our friends, a teacher, rates Arthur way above average in every department. He's working as an electrician, and studies evenings. Last week, just for the fun, we had him take a vocational guidance test, and if the result means anything, we have a modest young Edison in the family.

Believe me, Harry, it's a grand thing to see young fellows like our Arthur step out of a past full of bitterness and come to life anew, thanks to the warmth and friendships of a Jewish home. That alone has more than repaid us for the small adjustments we've had to make around the house. And when I think of what it's meant to us to have Arthur with us, I feel that we're the ones who should be the most grateful.

The difficulty of finding homes was compounded by the fact that the arrival of the orphans overlapped the new long-awaited immigration policy that finally permitted many more DP's to enter the country.

CHAPTER FIVE

The Search in Europe

THE CONTRAST between the European and Canadian operations of the Project was as wide as the ocean separating the Old and New Worlds. In Canada the Project unfolded according to the principles of modern organization. Congress established a hierarchy of command, delegating responsibility and setting up a system of accountability. Problems could be studied and solved in comfortable meeting rooms, and there was usually time to reflect and to talk over difficult problems with trusted friends during dinner or while taking a leisurely walk through a favourite park. Information could be sent out to people in the field using reliable telecommunication systems that were certain to deliver their messages in legible or audible form. And different forms of transportation were not only abundant but could be expected to run like clockwork.

Overseas, conditions were far different. Two years after the defeat of the Nazis, Europe was still digging itself out from the devastating effects of the War. Communications were difficult, rationing was still in force in many countries and the normal order of civil society was still trying to re-establish itself.

In July 1947 some 650,000 refugees—about 170,000 of them Jewish—were still living in the sixty camps and refugee centres supported in Western Europe by the United Nations Relief and Rehabilitation Administration. At the same time, many thousands of young people were still roaming around Europe, while others were temporarily sheltered in refugee camps waiting for some country to give them permission to enter. Among them were an estimated 4,000 Jewish children.

With the arrival of the Allied armies, these youngsters had emerged one by one from their hiding places—from forests, from monasteries and convents, from isolated and distant villages, from basements and nailed-up cupboards. Most were older and had survived concentration camps, for only those strong enough to work were allowed to live. In their search for parents, brothers and sisters, they had set out on a round of DP camps looking for members of their family who might have survived. Many who found no relatives couldn't be held back from returning to their countries of origin. They travelled on foot, hitched rides in jeeps and on trains, begged food from army units or lived a precarious existence on the profits of black market dealings in cigarettes and jewellery until they reached the places they had once known as home. They went through the ruins questioning town officials and people they remembered as neighbours. In most cases the search ended in vain. Once convinced that none of their family had survived they would drift back to displaced persons camps, like Prien and Aglasterhausen in the American zone of Germany.

Congress assigned three people the task of looking among this chaos for what they believed would be "the tens of thousands" of youngsters eligible for the Project. The three were Lottie Levinson and Ethel Ostry of Vancouver and Winnipeg respectively, and a German-Jewish refugee named Manfred Saalheimer. A fourth person, Greta Fischer, who had been stationed in Germany since 1945 providing services for children as a member of UNRRA Team 182, also became a key person in the European operations of the Project.

It is impossible to speak of refugees during that time without at least a glance at UNRRA, the greatest relief operation in history. On November 9, 1943 representatives of forty-four nations gathered around the table in the East Room at the White House in Washington when Allied victory in Europe and the Far East was slowly emerging. On that White House conference table lay the fate of millions of human beings in occupied lands as much as on each Allied tank and plane. The document they had come to sign established UNRRA, the first international relief agency in world history.

Its immediate antecedent, established by the League of Nations following World War I, was the High Commission for Refugees under the direction of Norwegian polar explorer, Fridtj Nansen. It was disbanded in December, 1938 when the numbers of refugees had become so great and conditions too precarious for the Commission to cope adequately with the situation. According to Gerald E. Dirks, "the most significant success achieved by the Commission was the development of a travel document to replace the traditional passports for stateless persons which expedited the movement of thousands of persecuted peoples across national frontiers."[1]

The Evian Conference which took place in July 1938 when thirty-two nations from Western Europe and the British Commonwealth met to find a solution for refugees, proved no more successful. Its sole accomplishment was the formation of a new Intergovernmental Committee on Refugees.

UNRRA was a unique experiment in international co-operation and marked the first time that the nations of the world would agree on the principle of working together in peace by pooling their resources to rescue and aid all victims of aggression, without political and economic bias. According to Michael R. Marrus, it was the first time in which Europe seriously addressed together a refugee crisis of international dimensions.[2]

At first, with the war still on, a welfare agency scheduled to go into operation in that remote period called "after the war" failed to stir any immediate interest. Preparations were made to deal with a great emergency by co-ordinating, and at times, financing relief and rehabilitation programs in the war-ravaged countries of Europe; and by repatriating civilians dislocated as a result of war. But the dimensions of the catastrophe and the unprecedented suffering of civilian populations were impossible to foresee. The extent of the distress and

Greta Fischer leading children to supper at the Kloster Indersdorf
United Nations Relief and Rehabilitation Administration's (UNRRA)
Children's Centre, Germany.
United Nations Archives

UNRRA Medical Welfare Officer Anne Marie Dewaal-Malefyt
and one of the nuns with a group of babies, at the UNRRA
Children's Centre, an old nunnery 25 miles north of Munich,
May 1946.
United Nations Archives

complexity of problems became known only when workers in the field saw it first-hand. All of the international resources were inadequate to relieve more than a fraction of the suffering.

UNRRA's original forty-four member states of the newly-created United Nations grew to forty-eight before its massive operation began in the second half of 1945. From the outset UNRRA was conceived as temporary and short-lived, lasting only until December 1946; but conditions remained in a state of severe crisis so that it wasn't until June 1947 that its major functions were taken over by the International Refugee Organizaton (IRO). The International Children's Emergency Fund (ICEF) and the World Health Organization were also offshoots of UNRRA.[3]

At its peak in mid-1946 UNRRA employed a staff of about 25,000 from thirty-three nationalities, making it the largest group of international civil servants ever assembled to work together. They operated in seventeen war-torn countries. The largest number of staff worked in Washington headquarters and in the European regional office located in London. In her personal papers Greta Fischer writes that the London-based operation was set up in a dozen buildings covering a square block which had been connected by tunnels to make for easy access from one building to another. It was located in a former residential area facing the bomb-damaged BBC. Smaller units functioned in the Missions of the receiving countries and in DP Camps and Assembly Centres in Germany, Austria, Italy, the Middle East and China.

Creating such a staff had been a monumental challenge. Recruiting was made difficult not only by the shortage of available personnel of all grades and skills, but also by the impossibility of planning and estimating requirements for an operation which had not yet taken definite shape. As the Allied Expeditionary Forces advanced in Europe in 1944 and the time for field operations approached, UNRRA established Citizens' Panels in various important cities in Canada as well as other countries to stimulate interest in UNRRA's recruiting campaign.

Many who answered the call were of exceptional ability and dedication. Among the ranks were specialists in administration, agriculture, civil and industrial engineering. Others included skilled practitioners in public health, medicine, and social welfare, while others had been academics before the war. What they all had in common was qualities of leadership and tremendous vitality that led them not only to work outrageous hours but to make other people proud to work alongside at their pace.[4]

This dedication is apparent in an anonymous note handwritten on a single sheet of faded blue paper, dated March 1944, found in Congress Archives. It was written by an UNRRA worker assigned to refugee children.

> Our UNRRA team started out with eight members of five different nationalities: English, French, Belgian, Luxembourgian and American. We grew to fifteen with members from Holland, Switzerland, Australia and Czechoslovakia. We worked with children of twenty-two different nationalities, not to mention those of unknown origin. As you know, I believed fervently in the theory of UNRRA when I joined, even though I had reservations about its practical application and great fears that it might be so restricted in its work that it could do little of real construction. One could not but appproach Europe with trepidation and wonder if people so deeply hurt could work for themselves, much less work together. And they could and did.
>
> We found the most incredible normalcy in response to proper treatment. The recuperative powers of the children were beyond our wildest hopes. I shall never be able to understand how youngsters who were ruthlessly torn from their parents, their homes, put to work at humiliating tasks, forced to lie and steal in order to survive—could adjust so readily. And if there was any special formula that we used it

was merely that we cared, that they knew we loved them, that we wanted and worked to achieve the same goals—the search for relatives, good food, decent clothes, education, and emigration.

Of the original three members of Congress' War Orphans' Team in Europe, only Manfred Saalheimer did not first pass through the ranks of UNRRA. He held a doctorate in law from a German university, and had come to Canada as an interned refugee, one of the 2,290 "enemy aliens" sent to Farnham, Quebec by the British government in 1940. Upon his release from internment, Saalheimer took on a number of administrative and educational functions at Congress, often acting as assistant to Saul Hayes.

In a letter dated September 9, 1947 to Saul Hayes at Congress headquarters in Montreal, Dr. Saalheimer defined a two-fold role for himself.

> To see for myself what kind of children may be available for Canada, and secondly, to act as a liaison between Congress and other organizations involved. I had also the mission to set up the machinery by which the movement could function in such a way as to allow proper control for Congress.[5]

Saalheimer arrived in Europe—England being his first stop—with high optimism. He was encouraged to find that the Department of Immigration had already notified its overseas agencies of the general outline of the Project and left the working out of the details to his discretion in co-operation with the officers concerned. His dealings with the Canadian European Emigration head office at Sackville House in London went smoothly, and so certain was he of accomplishing his mission that before leaving for Paris he finalized arrangements with the Cunard White Star Line for a number of children's groups on several sailings of the *Aquitania*.

Arriving in Paris with a plan worked out in detail including transportation for the children, Saalheimer was confident of smooth sailing ahead. He was caught completely off guard by what he was told by the Jewish organizations—few children would be available, no more than 100, at most 150. "Few Jewish children under eighteen were alive."

Over those first few weeks in Europe Saalheimer learned just how ruthless the German campaign of murder against Jewish children had been. He was also to learn that many of the children who survived owed their lives to the Christian parents who had sheltered them by claiming them as their own. Understandably few of these foster parents were willing to give up their children.

Saalheimer was not deterred from his mission and set to work at once. He contacted the Joint Distribution Committee (JDC) offices across Europe. JDC is a major agency established by American Jewry for the relief of distressed Jews in foreign countries. It was very active in starting programmes for children: child care centres, rehabilitation and training schools, medical clinics and hospitals for sick children. He interviewed UNRRA field officers as they came through the Paris office; he addressed a meeting of the Hebrew Immigrant Aid Society (HIAS) representatives from sixteen European countries, and executive officers at IRO headquarters in Paris and Geneva. He travelled widely, functioning as Congress' eyes and ears in Europe.

It soon became apparent to Dr. Saalheimer that Congress had been wrong in thinking that one thousand Jewish orphans, eighteen years of age and younger, could be quickly found and their passage to Canada swiftly expedited. What he had been told earlier was confirmed— there were very few young children. Most had been killed by the Nazis. Moreover, many young people who could have met the requirements of the Canadian Project had been taken under the wing of Zionist organizations, who would consider nothing but taking them to Palestine where they believed the children belonged. At the same time eligible teenage survivors from the Iron Curtain countries who might have wanted to emigrate to Canada were not granted exit permits.

Countries like Poland, Romania and Hungary resisted losing their young citizens to the capitalist world. As a result, only those young people who were free to move but could not bear to enter yet another war zone, Palestine, moved from pillar to post in the British and American zones until they met up with the Congress War Orphans' Movement to Canada.

Operating out of JDC European Headquarters in Paris, among Saalheimer's tasks was the completion of the dossiers of all the children identified as eligible for the Canadian project. This meant writing the case histories of children who, in many instances, had brought with them the scantiest fragments of background information. In addition, each dossier had to have some documentation in lieu of birth certificates which were rarely available since records of birth had been destroyed, or religious origins deliberately falsified by parents before they were taken to concentration camps. Furthermore, each child had to provide proof that he was a "full orphan."

Like the anonymous UNRRA worker cited above, Saalheimer was caught up emotionally in the job before him. In an excerpt from a letter he wrote to Congress headquarters on December 23, 1947 he stated:

> I wish I could describe adequately how much this opportunity means to so many of the youth who are now waiting in DP camps. The ambition with which the boys look forward to their new life makes me realize what a godsend this youth project is for our young men. But we are hard put when we must rule out a boy because we find that he is over-age or that he has a surviving parent.
>
> One of the pathetic sights I witnesed recently was in Camp Adriatica, Italy. I was in the office of the Director of the camp discussing our procedures in the verification of birth and orphan status when a young man broke into the office and

urged that he be included in the scheme. This lad, though no more than five feet tall and looking quite youthful was older than eighteen. I do hope that at some time in the near future Canada may open its doors to other young men between the ages of eighteen and twenty-one, or at least to the brothers and sisters of those who have already been admitted to Canada.

Saalheimer had put his finger on another sore point between Congress and the Canadian government. The qualifying terms of the order-in-council had been more restrictive than Congress had originally wished. In initial conversations Hayes had hoped to convince the government to allow minors, defined in Canadian law as those under twenty-one years of age, to enter under the definition of orphan children.

"Our argument here," Hayes had explained to officials in a letter on April 30, 1947 "was that the children whom we wished to take care of five years ago are now by the passage of time 18, 19, 20 and 21." In response the Government did stretch the upper age limit to eighteen from sixteen, but the inclusion of their older brothers or sisters, who would have been enormous emotional support, was rejected.

When Congress' leaders were certain that only by raising the upper age limit could they find sufficient numbers of orphans they tried again and again to persuade the government to modify the qualifications. It was a heartbreaking prospect that after waiting so long for official permission, they would not be able to fill the allotted quota. Despite Congress' entreaties, the federal government remained firm.

In the Public Archives[6] an item dated January 1948 reveals the government's intransigent thinking:

Congress informs us that according to the present estimate overseas staff will be able to recruit only about 700 orphans under the age of eighteen and states that the staff has registered a certain number of brothers and sisters and cousins of eligible orphans who constitute the latter's only remaining kin but who are left behind because they are above the age of eighteen years. [Congress] states it would be highly desirable to preserve these family units by permitting these relatives to come to Canada.

They further state that in the DP camps there are many young people between the ages of eighteen and twenty-one fully orphaned who would make excellent material for Canadian immigration and request that order-in-council P.C.1647 be amended to include fully orphaned Jewish children between the ages of eighteen and twenty-one, stating that they would give preference to those living in DP camps who have brothers and sisters under the age of eighteen or some interested party in Canada. *This is really a request to extend the age of admissable orphaned children from eighteen to twenty-one years.*

The basis for the scheme was to save children and I therefore think that extending the age limit to twenty-one is going beyond what was intended. Further, the plan was for the children to be adopted and there would of course be no adoption in the bringing to Canada young people over eighteen years. I recommend that the original arrangement stand.

When the Project ended Saalheimer returned to his former activities at Congress. He died in 1967.

It would be hard to find a greater contrast—in life experience though not in dedication—to Manfred Saalheimer than the second Congress field worker, Lottie Levinson. Her involvement with the War Orphans Project began quite by chance.

I was working as a secretary at the Jewish Community Centre in Vancouver, quite liking my job, when Saul Hayes came to Vancouver. This was the last stop on his journey across

Canada organizing communities to help refugees. As a woman in my thirties I hadn't yet ventured far from home, in fact, I don't know that I had even set foot outside of British Columbia, not unusual for the times, I suppose. Anyway, I was much affected by what Mr. Hayes said and the "straight from the heart" way in which he said it. I had thought a bit about the enormous help that was needed, but it wasn't until I heard Hayes in person that I could imagine the huge scale of the need. When he encouraged us to work for Congress I applied without really understanding what I was applying for. So it took me by great surprise to be hired as a European field worker and sent immediately overseas seconded to UNRRA's refugee programme. I felt utterly unprepared.[7]

UNRRA's training procedures were very basic compared to today's standards. Most Canadian trainees went to College Park at the University of Maryland, UNRRA's American training centre which had opened in May 1944. At first the course was eight weeks long, but increasing pressure from the field reduced it to two weeks. From there they were sent for further training to a facility on the Normandy coast in France at the seaside town of Granville, where UNRRA field workers from all countries received their induction—more of a joke than anything else, according to Levinson. However, Woodbridge in *The History of UNRRA* reports on the training at Granville in this way:

> There can be little doubt that the training provided for field staff was of value. It could have been more useful if circumstances had permitted attendance at the courses to be more complete, if more instructors with field experience had been available and if the staff had not been handicapped by never knowing when courses would be broken up because unexpectedly early development of travel opportunities prematurely took "students" away.

Children leave a transit centre enroute to Kloster Indersdorf
Children's Centre, May 1946.
United Nations Archives

New arrivals at the Children's Centre get fitted for clothes.
Most of them arrived with just the clothes on their backs.
Acme photo by Haacker, United Nations Archives

All were housed in the Hotel Normandy, once one of the most luxurious hotels in Europe but now showing signs of a grim past—it had been used as a German headquarters and the top floor had been a torture chamber. Later it had become Eisenhower's headquarters, and then it was taken over by UNRRA. One former field worker from British Columbia, the late Marion Pennington, told the author that her strongest memory of training was being instructed in the use of a DDT spray gun: "Up women's skirts, down men's trousers," she said. A public health nurse by profession, Mrs. Pennington added, "I shudder to think of the harm we may have done."

Given her experience as an UNRRA worker and the fact that she was already in Europe when permission for the orphans was granted, Levinson was well-positioned to carry out the crucial assignment of overseeing the required documentation. Tasks included assembling a social history in duplicate; collecting X-rays and blood test results, and acquiring certification in lieu of birth certificates as proof of orphanhood.

Every part of the operation had its own hazards which could result in a youngster's rejection by the Canadian authorities. There was always the fear that someone's documents would be found unacceptable because of a missing bit of information or as a result of some official's idiosyncrasies. Forty-five years later, in our interview, her voice was still full of indignation as she spoke of it:

> The examining doctors were a constant stumbling block.
> They always managed to find something wrong. It was either
> a spot on an X-ray indicating TB or signs of glaucoma. And
> sometimes it was an imaginary speck. I learned quickly how
> to read X-rays. The doctors were even known to diagnose
> "illiteracy" in the youth who had spent their childhoods in
> concentration camps—as a medical reason for ineligibility to
> immigrate to Canada.

Levinson couldn't emphasize strongly enough how important personality was in getting things done. "If you knew your way around people in positions of power," she said, "half the battle was won. If you didn't have that talent, you were lost. Fortunately, for the work I was sent overseas to do, I was well-endowed with that attribute."

Levinson became widely recognized in many parts of the world for her more than three decades of outstanding service to displaced Jewish people of Europe. As countries softened their policies of admitting refugees Levinson lost no time in contacting consulates, ambassadors, and people in positions of power who could help displaced persons. In the latter part of her career she was associated with the Jewish Distribution Committee and the Hebrew Immigrant Aid Society. She retired and returned to Vancouver in 1976 where she died in 1989.

The third person employed by Congress in Europe was Ethel Ostry. At the time of the passing of Privy Council Order 1647, she was Director of a large UNRRA displaced persons centre at Hohenfeld, Germany—an already huge task which expanded greatly when she was asked by Congress to take on responsibility for the Canadian War Orphans Project. Unlike her two counterparts, she left a copious record of her work in the refugee camps. Her detailed weekly reports to Congress Headquarters in Montreal, as well as her unpublished memoirs, entitled "Where is My Family?" give a full account of her activities in the refugee camps.[8] She also left hundreds of photographs of the individual refugees she was responsible for. Given the onerous demands of her assignment, the fact that she found the energy to record with such exactitude the events of her days tells much about Ostry's character.

Winnipeg-born, her education and professional career had prepared her well to carry out Congress' mandate. A graduate of the University of Manitoba, and the Montreal School of Social Work before the Project was launched, she was well-known and widely respected for her directorship of the Jewish Family Welfare Departments, first in Montreal and later in Toronto. Congress made an excellent choice in assigning her to the European operation of the Project. An energetic, athletic woman she carried authority comfortably.

Ostry had become interested in left-wing politics at an early age and throughout her life remained committed to her strong political beliefs. Not only an outspoken supporter of progressive ideas, she was also ready to act on them. With the formation of the Canadian Commonwealth Federation (CCF) party she moved to Saskatchewan to contribute to the development of social programs. In addition to earning respect for her competence, Ostry soon developed a reputation for not brooking interference or opposition kindly. She was a suitable person for Congress to assign the task of working out the details of assembling the children once it was determined that they had met the terms of the order-in-council.

In one of her earliest reports to Congress, written soon after she was appointed to the Project, Ostry described her activities and the difficulties encountered:

> On Aug. 26 immediately on my return to Munich I set up office in Munich-Passing, room 4, 20 Bismarckstr. and went about the selection of children who might go on the first transport of Sept. 13 and the following one on Oct. 1. I had selected forty-two children at Prien Children's Centre whom I intended to recommend to the Canadian immigration officials. The Canadian team was asked to visit Prien and consider visas for these children in early Sept. Mr. Cormier expressed, in very unfriendly terms, reluctance to give these children immediate attention, saying that he had received no instructions from his government in this matter.
>
> Some weeks later a Canadian immigration team consisting of Mr. Lamont (Consul), several security officers and doctors, and a number of representatives of the Labour Department, as well as my good friend Charley Grant, arrived in the Munich area. I took the opportunity to explain the problem in regard

to the children. Mr. Lamont gave me his promise to consider the children in Prien in a few days. Then, whether intentionally or not, he and the doctor went to Prien without my knowing anything about it. As soon as I heard about it from the director of the centre, I got there as quickly as I could. But I was without proper transportation and had to rely on an old jeep.

As luck would have it I arrived in Prien after the Team had left. The children, in the meantime, had all been questioned by the security officer in a truly RCMP fashion. He had passed twenty-seven of the group, including ironically, a one-year-old. Many in the group had been rejected by the doctor because the X-ray films taken of the children at Altersheim Hospital were of paper and not film, and under no circumstances would he bend. The hospital lacked film and the Canadian doctor would not agree that the paper film was equally good.

On another occasion Ostry had to deal with the rejection of children because it was discovered by the examining doctor that ten of the children had X-ray films that were outdated by two months, and that the Wasserman tests, though in order, were duplicates rather than originals, and therefore not acceptable.

She managed to convince the Director of Altersheim Hospital to obtain large film for the re-evaluation in accordance with Canadian standards, and Heilbronn Hospital for repeat Wassermans. But that wasn't the only problem.

Mr. Lamont with the assistance of two newly arrived vice-consuls considered the applications of forty children. I presented the children with all the necessary information findings. Mr. Lamont's attitude toward the children was not unfriendly, but for each applicant I had to direct entreaties regarding age limit and appeal for those within a few days of the date on which they were interviewed. I had also to repeatedly assure him that all efforts have been made since liberation to trace parents and that those recommended were full orphans. I believe in the end they accepted my explanations.

In addition, it was hoped that the government would not prove so inflexible in demanding verifiable evidence that a given child was indeed an orphan. Some children could never supply proof due to the difficulties of actually determining which parents are alive and which are not.

The question of proof of orphan status was therefore left vague, but as Levinson remembered that didn't reduce suspicions. Everybody who worked in the refugee camps, she asserted, knew that incoming mail was furtively opened by camp officials fearing that an orphan had concealed the survival of a parent in order to qualify. As soon as one problem was cleared away another would appear. At one point Ostry was following up the case of a young German Jew named Chaim, only to find that the Canadian officials had the impression that German Jews were not eligible for immigration. Luckily, Ostry knew that Chaim had been born in Luxembourg, and was able to convince the officials that the youngster was eligible. That incident occurred in September 1947, early in her work for the Project; she concluded her report by stating, "I now have some experience and a better understanding of the Canadian requirements and expect that things will go more smoothly."

That was not to be; each report described a new set of obstacles. A major one occurred four months later because of the Canadian team's disorganization; the team was unable or unwilling to specify a date and place for considering the orphans' visas. Writing as if no one would believe such a story unless she wrote it in log form, detail-by-detail, or needing to write to be sure herself that it had actually happened, Ostry recounts how at six a.m. on a cold January day she set off from the Aglasterhausen refugee centre with thirty-one children in her charge, travelling in one ambulance and an open truck. They arrived in the Stuttgart transit centre four hours later, frozen and exhausted, but in time to keep their appointment with the Canadian immigration team. They waited all morning. No team appeared. After making enquiries Ostry was told that Mr. Potvin, the team leader, had not returned from vacation and that Dr. Sadowski, who was reported to be ill, was still in London. Ostry pleaded with them to send another doctor to examine the children as soon as possible.

In the meantime Ostry had thirty-one youngsters to look after while they waited for a new appointment. The most pressing need was to find beds and blankets for the children at the transit centre, as well as food to supplement the meagre rations of weak potato soup and black coffee which were available there. At the Army Post Exchange she managed to purchase, "as expensive as it was," towels, soap, biscuits, candy and cheese. Nothing seemed to be working in their favour, not even the NFB film which she had brought to show the children. It did not fit the projector on the premises. The one comforting constant, writes Ostry, "was that in spite of the hardships, the children were wonderful, and prepared to undergo any hardship at the least chance of having an opportunity to come before the team."

The following morning everyone was up early awaiting the arrival of Mr. Potvin and the doctor, but nobody showed up. It turned out that Mr. Potvin was still in Heidelberg and there was no word from Dr. Sadowski. Ostry happened to know another doctor in Stuttgart, and was able to talk him into coming to examine the children. It later turned out that Dr. Sadowski had long since returned from London and was simply waiting for Mr. Potvin to call him.

Ostry signed off on a typically optimistic note that a new man, Mr. Bird, was coming to head the Canadian team, and that she expected greater progress could be made. But four days later she wrote that although she was pleased that the processing of the children with the immigration team was going more smoothly, it was now the security officer, Mr. Siren, who was holding things up. He could not be

Ethel Ostry in Europe, 1947 or 1948. Ostry was assigned
responsibility for the European operations of the War
Orphans Project by the Canadian Jewish Congress.
Canadian Jewish Congress National Archives

A dormitory at Kloster Indersdorf, Germany.
Acme photo, United Nations Archives

convinced, even after being shown a letter from the Department of Mines and Resources, that security screening for children under eighteen was not required. That meant Ostry had to present each applicant herself, which would take several days. And this at a time when applications were coming to her in such great numbers that she could hardly keep up with the demand, not to mention working without any administrative staff.

As the months progressed the pressure of work intensified as the urgency to leave Germany increased. Moreover, the Canadian investigators seemed to be getting tougher. Ostry noted "an attitude of antagonism and searching for flaws is very evident." Relations with Canadian officials became particularly tense when refugee workers were accused of being deceitful. At one point she received complaints that orphans she had recommended were not of the required ages— the dates of birth had obviously been altered. After a thorough enquiry Ostry found the root of the problem. The young applicants had changed the ages on their forms themselves in order to be old enough to receive cigarette rations in the camp. No one had thought to verify.

Not all of the problems came from Europe; Congress too could make life difficult for its workers. In a June 1948 report to Congress Ostry acknowledged that it had become impossible to continue to work alone and asked for assistance. But even that supposedly simple request was not easily filled. She had arranged for Miss Eva Kraft to be released from her position with the International Refugees Organization (IRO) and had already learned that if Congress was not able to pay the monthly allotment of $35, Kraft was prepared to forego this amount. But approval was needed from Congress Headquarters in Montreal. In the end Ostry's request was granted, but only for a short period of two months.

The location from which Ostry was to identify children eligible for Canada was UNRRA's single International Centre for children, Kloster Indersdorf. It was there that the last of the Project's key European workers, Greta Fischer, was working for UNRRA Team 182 when the order-in-council was passed.

Like Manfred Saalheimer, Greta Fischer was a refugee herself. Seventeen years old when the Germans invaded her native Czechoslovakia, Greta managed to escape at the last moment to find safety in England, where she worked as a nanny, the only work permitted her as a refugee. By chance the medical couple who employed Greta recognized her many talents in caring for their young children and recommended her to Anna Freud who was looking for staff. It was at this time that Freud, and Dorothy Burlingham, were establishing the wartime nurseries in Hampstead to provide care for children separated from their parents. It was from observations made at this nursery that Freud drew important scientific conclusions about child development. These later became the cornerstone of her germinal studies in child development which set the stage for modern child psychology.

Working with Freud offered Greta an ideal opportunity to study the advantages and disadvantages of various types of institutional care. Since the nursery was established to serve children as well as study them, there was no better training for Greta's later work with UNRRA's Children's Centre. The primary goals of Freud's program were to repair damage caused by war conditions, and to prevent further harm.

In 1944 when Greta learned that UNRRA was looking for child experts to form a special unit to go to Germany after the war to rescue displaced children, she "just had to go." Greta applied and was chosen on the spot and assigned to Team 182.

When UNRRA Team 182 arrived in Germany a year later in the middle of June 1945, smoke was still curling from the blasted ruins, and the roads were often impassable because of endless columns of barefoot, unfed refugees. Dressed in battle dress and driving army lorries, the Team reached its destination just behind the American army. They would have been indistinguishable from the American soldiers were it not for the bold white UNRRA letters embossed on the scarlet shoulder flashes stitched on their shoulders and caps. They had come to probe the desolation in search of a new kind of debris of modern war—displaced and stolen children. No one knew where or how many children there were. The only certainty was that there were thousands, or tens of thousands, of non-German children lost in the chaos.

In UNRRA's records these children are sometimes referred to as the "unattached children," at other times as the "unaccompanied or stolen children." No one could agree on a word to name a condition so bizarre. Some had been taken from families in the occupied countries and sent to Germany to be indoctrinated as Germans. Whole classrooms of children had been boarded onto buses and told they were being taken on a holiday. These were also the children of forced labourers who were not permitted to keep them, as well as Jewish children who had survived the war in hiding or had been liberated from concentration and labour camps.

The sixteenth century monastery of Kloster Indersdorf, ten kilometers from Dachau, was converted into UNRRA's only International Children's Centre. Over its front door the grim philosophy of its founding order, the Augustine monks, was still legible—*Liebe ist staerker als der Tod* (love is stronger than death). Given that children's needs would require frequent consultation, UNRRA Team 182 had chosen to locate in the village of Indersdorf in order to allow easy access to UNRRA and U.S. Military Headquarters in nearby Munich. However practical this arrangement may have been in obtaining basic supplies from the American forces, it proved useless in filling requisitions for badly needed baby bottles, toilet training potties, clothing and other supplies needed for children.

Word spread quickly throughout Germany that a home for children had been created. In a steady stream, desperately needy children came to its doors. They ranged in age from two to eighteen, were from twenty-four different nationalities and many different backgrounds. A large number were found by the American military or by UNRRA personnnel working in the field and brought to Kloster Indersorf, which at once became a "children's clearing house." Others arrived at odd hours after making their way to Indersdorf on their own. Whatever the hour, the slightest drumming of small fists on that ancient door would bring Greta running from her bed down the winding, creaking stairs and along the drafty corridors. Pushing open the heavy door she would often find shivering in its shadow young orphans looking up at her with frightened and searching eyes.

During our interviews, Greta's face glowed as she remembered the children:

> We were everything to those children. But beyond everything—mother, father, doctor, nurse and teacher—we knew that a vital part of our work was to help the children talk about what had happened to them. Millions of unrepeatable stories, stories of pain and suffering that the mind could not comprehend—we knew that these stories had to come out. We also felt a strong responsibiity to history and recorded as many of the children's stories as possible. In order to do this we had to function with just the right amalgam of bravery and numbness. To cry with the children would not have helped them. Being so busy every minute of the day helped to keep us normal.

Team 182 and the children had expected their stay at Kloster Indersdorf to be short, a routine processing step before moving on homeward or to new lands. And for the fortunate ones their stay was brief. But for the Jewish children there were no homes to return to and no new lands wanted them. For those who shrank from living again behind barbed wire in Palestine, Kloster Indersdorf was the one place that would have them.

Visiting Kloster Indersdorf soon after the arrival of forty Jewish children, in November 1948 Ostry submitted this report to

Upon arrival at Kloster Indersdorf Children's Centre,
the baggage of two Polish children–a brother and sister–
is examined by Greta Fischer for means of identification,
March 1946.
United Nations Archives

The older DP orphans at the Kloster Indersdorf Children's
Centre found time to care for the younger DP's—a diversion
from memories of Nazi concentration camps.
Photo by Maxine Rude, United Nations Archives

headquarters:

> The physical needs of the children seemed to be well met in this cold, musty-smelling cloister in its beautiful surroundings. But when I asked the director what plans were being made for the Jewish children's future I was met with unusual vagueness and told what he considered a good joke. When the Soviet liaison officer, according to custom, had written his name in the guest book at the conclusion of his visit he had written in big letters on a new page: This institution is spreading anti-Soviet propaganda among the children.

And in another report to UNRRA Headquarters someone had described it "as the kind of building that would result if so many rooms were tossed up in a blanket and allowed to settle."

Team 182 used all of its ingenuity to restore some semblance of normal childhood life. Rooms were cleared and turned into classrooms, sewing rooms built for making clothing for the children, and gardens tended. When fabric appropriate for children's garments could not be supplied by the U.S. army, bales of red flag material that had been stockpiled by Nazis in deserted barns were converted into toddlers' overalls and blouses for the older girls.

But for all the encouragement and care that was given the children, the Kloster could at best produce only an artificial security. Every villager on the street was seen as a killer or an accomplice in the murder of their parents and the older boys and girls could not suppress their hatred. Daily life had to be contained within the walls of the monastery, except for occasional trips to Munich for special events. The orphans were desperate to leave Germany.

Unfortunately, as had been the case with Canada, the nations which had defeated Germany were reluctant to open their doors to the youngest victims. Forty-five years later, remembering the western nations' attitude toward "her children" Greta Fischer's fury remained full-blown as she retold the story:

For the two long years of 1945 to 1947, we pleaded, we waited, we tried to convince the world of the Jewish children's membership in the human race. But the world remained closed to these children and nobody wanted them. Each nation was fearful that the children would be so damaged that they could never be assimilated into normal life and would always be a burden on the state. By the time Canada's offer came we had almost reached the point of complete despair.

Each month's delay due to bureaucratic cancellations faced by Ethel Ostry and Lottie Levinson brought with it the eighteenth birthday of some of the orphans, a happy event in other circumstances but a cruel blow in this situation because it meant the orphans were no longer eligible to enter Canada under the Project. Years later, Greta could still recall the heart-breaking words of those rejected for this reason.

"We lost our parents, we lost our sisters and brothers, our homes and everything precious to us. Now we get punished again."

The first offer to accept a small group of children came from France; followed soon after by Sweden, and later by the Canadian War Orphans Project.

The orphans arrived in Canada at irregular intervals, often with little advance warning or after unexpected delays, from September 1947 until January 1949. In that month, after many false starts, the last group arrived in New York aboard the Polish ship, *S.S. Rodnick*. They included twenty youngsters from Kloster Indersdorf, the last children from there, accompanied by Greta Fischer. On reaching the United States they were hastily placed on a sealed train as "dangerous cargo." Only then were they allowed to complete their journey to Montreal and Toronto.

But bureaucratic blunders continued in Canada. Greta and the twenty young people arrived as though "we were like one family and I needed them as much as they me," but they were separated. Somebody, somewhere, in trying to make some order out of the mass of documentation and confusing plans had assigned Greta to Montreal, and the youngsters to Toronto. However hard she tried to get herself transferred to Toronto, nothing worked in her favour. She had no choice but to devote herself to caring for the children already in residence at the Montreal Reception Home where she was given a position.

For all the preparation described both in Canada and Europe, it was only the first step. The real task of placing and looking after the children with individual families now loomed in front of the Jewish community. What sort of task was it and how did they see it in the light of their own circumstances? And what would be its victories and its defeats?

Bath time with UNRRA child specialist Greta Fischer. May 1946.
United Nations Archives

CHAPTER SIX

Arrival and Reception

As soon as one problem was resolved another was sure to take its place. The largest number of young people—798—were sent to Montreal and Toronto. Unlike the smaller cities where the orphans were placed immediately in homes, the leaders of the Project agreed that a waiting period in some type of reception centre was necessary. At the same time everyone was determined to avoid creating what could become permanent institutions for a core of unplaced orphans.

In Toronto the Reception Centre was housed in the former Jewish library at Harbord and Markham Streets, about a half a mile from the YMHA. The former Director of the Centre, Dr. Joseph Klinghofer, previously a professor of modern languages and literature in Poland, described his function with amusement as having been "partly educator and partly janitor" to the orphans who lived in the Centre, forty to fifty at a time. Now in his middle eighties, this soft-spoken scholar resides in a modest, book-lined house on a quiet Toronto street. His former charges speak of him with great reverence.

Dr. Klinghofer underscores with philosophic irony the diverse roles history cast for him. In a mock confessional tone he recounts how he entered Canada under false pretenses, the only way possible at the time. In order to qualify under the new immigration labour policy he had to pretend to be a tailor. After surviving the war working for the Polish underground as a BBC translator, he made his way to a DP camp in Austria where he found work with the International Refugee Organization (IRO), and later the Hebrew Immigrant Aid Society

(HIAS). He was then delegated as secretary to Max Entin, chairman of the Commission for the selection of needle trade workers for Canada, who befriended and encouraged him to apply for immigration.

Dr. Klinghofer, a man who spoke eight languages fluently and read two others— picked his words with the care of someone searching for a secure foothold on a hazardous mountain climb. Taking as much time as he needed, he would not move to a new subject until he first found the precise words to express his thoughts. The long pauses that punctuated his speech were set by a metre that recognized no audience. One can easily imagine the unwavering sincerity of this man directed to the young refugees under his care.

> My job was not easy. It was made the more difficult because I often had to take the orphans' side and quarrel with the social workers who tended to present reality very harshly. They of course had their own agenda to follow. I had much compassion for those children because, to some extent, they had been misled in the refugee camps. I understood their psychology better. But there were some social workers, especially Rose Wolfe, now Chancellor of Toronto University, who tried not to be bookish, and shared my sentiments.

Reaching back in time Dr. Klinghofer slowly shifted position and eased himself deeper into his armchair. As he spoke of the young people's states of mind an unmistakable sadness crept into his voice and eyes, and one sensed the source of his deep understanding. Was he speaking as much about his own disappointment and hardships as the boys' and girls' when he said the following?

> There was a tremendous gap between the hopes of these young people and the realities of Canadian life. For one thing, their will to survive was made possible by the hope that once

peace came, the world would make up for their sufferings and all their dreams would come true. They expected to be received with open arms and to be compensated for their losses. Also, they had been fed the idea that they were coming to a golden land, and that they would be adopted by rich families who would give them the opportunity to study in high school and go on to university. The reality was different. Very few were adopted, and in many cases the adoptions didn't work out well. For most of them life in Canada meant being assigned to a home where they were given room and board, and sent for training or work in manual occupations.

Applying the insights of the teacher he was, Dr. Klinghofer used many educational methods to "lead them away from their realms of fantasy towards seeing the realities of life in Canada." He accomplished this by inviting rabbis, lawyers, business people, and others to the Centre to speak about the hardships of their younger years and to tell how hard they had to work until they slowly made progress. The question and answer periods were a very important part. "We also tried to cheer them up and to soften their disappointments by introducing musical hours and, whenever possible, obtained tickets for them to attend concerts."

Not one to dwell on personal hardship, Dr. Klinghofer, admitted his work was hard and his days fourteen to sixteen hours long. "I couldn't rest until all the young boys and girls were back from going out to shows, and some of them were wild. There was also such a mixture: some were liberal and others orthodox, always finding fault with the kashruth of the Centre.

Dr. Klinghofer recounted how the issues around religious observances were a source of constant conflict between the orthodox and the less observant. Insignificant as it may sound from this perspective in time, the use of the record player on the Sabbath became a hotly contested issue. Instead of allowing the matter to remain within the confines of the Centre, the devout orphans established contact with orthodox elements in the city, who in turn exerted pressure on the leadership of Congress to institute a regime of strict Sabbath observance. Ordinarily this body would have treated the question as a minor problem, quite remote from the larger policy issues with which it was concerned, but because of the pressure the record player was silenced over the strenuous protests of the non-orthodox youth.

As a mark of pride in his youngsters's many accomplishments coupled with the personal self-satisfaction at having done his very best in spite of the obstacles, Dr. Klinghoffer unself-consciously declared:

> Somehow all these matters were overcome with patience. And one thing was clear—overcoming disaster had created in these young people an inner well of energy that served them well in their push to better positions and to achievement. They wanted to make it, and most did. Surprisingly, there were only one or two cases of mental breakdown.
>
> What makes their story remarkable is that the inner mechanism of energy these youth acquired trying to overcome disaster, later served them in their pursuit of accomplishment. Their ambitions were nourished by a dream world which would bring them the riches that would release them forever from the starvation and pains they had known. The inner mechanism of their minds was to want more, to work harder to get it, and to always move forward. They took with them from the netherworld where everything good had been denied them the knowledge that you had to work for your own miracles.

Dr. Klinghofer could not end without acknowledging the role of the community, asserting that whenever there was a special need the community came and helped.

People may have been disappointed by the behaviour of the orphans, who were often arrogant and demanding, but throughout the Project they remained extremely touched by the fate of these young people and helped them whenever they could.

Rose Wolfe, Dr. Klinghofer's former valued fellow-worker, relates her own memories. Seated in the Chancellor's regally appointed black and gold office, a woman full of good cheer and high energy, she was eager to recall her days as a young, inexperienced social worker assigned to the War Orphans Project as a foster homefinder and caseworker. She refers to the experience as the most "formative" in her life.

Wolfe had heard about war orphans, but not being connected to the Jewish community at the time, she was not particularly aware of what was happening. She believes that might have been partly because it was treated like a big secret. "Certainly no one in the larger community knew about it," she explains, "which is not surprising given that the Jewish community was surrounded by widespread anti-semitism, and as a result did everything to avoid being noticed. 'Sha shtill (keep a low profile) was the prevailing code."

Three incidents stand out in Wolfe's memory. First, she often wonders what happened eventually to the four young Belgian boys she knew who never spoke and never laughed. Second, she shudders to think how little she and her fellow workers knew then about how to deal with anger. In particular, she regrets as a terrible mistake in one placement with which she was involved.

A bitter, sullen girl full of rage, for whom nothing we did was good enough, we committed to the Clark Institute of Psychiatry. It upset the whole community and led to a revolt by her foster family, who withdrew her from the hospital and severed all contact with us.

And lastly, Wolfe will never forget the many happy outcomes she witnessed. In doing a follow-up visit to enquire how things were going with one placement she asked whether Sylvia was co-operating with her foster family by doing her share of household tasks. She was told in a severe tone that a " young, pretty girl has better things to do than getting red hands washing dishes."

She too remembers the emotional outpouring of good will triggered by the call for homes, and fifty years later is almost incredulous at how highly motivated and well-intentioned people then were.

In his study, *The Redeemed Children*, Ben Lappin also stressed how the implementation of the Project was marked by spontaneous acts of kindness by families. The people who drove the orphans from place to place, he wrote, took them shopping, and even came to the Reception Centre to clean their rooms and make their beds, were the very community leaders who had formulated the policies for the Project. Not infrequently, a busy manufacturer, lawyer or auditor would begin a demanding day at the office after spending a good part of the previous night at the railway depot waiting "for the kids." And often business engagements would be abruptly terminated with the explanation that an appointment with "the kids" had to be kept. It wasn't long before the term "kids" needed no further explanation; people came to understand that the reference was to the war orphans and it was assumed that "the kids" came first. That these children were their first contact with the remnants of the destroyed Jewish community was always uppermost in people's thoughts.

It was not only the Jewish community who helped. The Toronto Board of Education provided special classes, and trade unions, employers, doctors, dentists, and many others offered needed services.

In the opinion of Moniek Lewkowitz there was no better beginning for life in Canada.

Unlike what happened to young refugees who went to the
U.S. and found themselves separated and [alone, spread out]

in all directions, we were much better off because we were able to stay together. I guess the Americans thought that was the fastest way to assimiliation. Maybe those kids did learn to speak English faster than we did, but we had the special advantage of belonging to a group. Can you imagine what that meant to us?

Also Toronto was a smaller city than those in the U.S., which enabled us to keep in touch with one another more easily. And even years after we moved out of the Centre, we would always gravitate back to College Street after work because we knew that we would always meet someone we knew there. We not only stuck together for moral support but we helped each other in all kinds of tangible ways—whether a loan of a few dollars to meet some emergency or to start some small business enterprise. The amounts at the time were trifling, but you can't measure something like that. Many of those friendships have lasted a lifetime.

Planning for the care of the European youngsters in Montreal followed in much the same way as in Toronto. In Montreal it was the second floor of the Herzl Medical Dispensary on Jeanne Mance Street, albeit small in size for the purpose, which was chosen as the most suitable location for a Reception Centre. Its proximity to the fine recreational facilities of the older YMHA on Mount Royal Avenue, the focal point for cultural and social life of Jewish Montreal, made it particularly desirable.

The "White House"—a large, luxurious mansion decorated with crystal chandeliers, flocked red wallpaper, and long stately driveway would certainly have appealed to some. Encircled and hidden by a tall, thick hedge on heavily trafficked Côte-de-Lièsse Road, it was discarded for reasons other than its distance from the centre of the city. Everybody at the time knew the "White House" was a gambling casino modeled on Las Vegas. It was so successful that people from

New York, and as far away as California came to try their hand at one of the specialties of the house—the dice and card game known as "barbotte"—as well as to partake of the fine food and drink. It was owned and operated by Harry Ship, whose short black hair and conservative business suits gave him more of the appearance of the accountant it was believed he once was, rather than the feared captain of the gambling world of Montreal. Ship was also known to be a most generous donor not only to community causes, but also to businessmen in financial trouble. However inapppropriate the proposal, the fact that the "White House" was considered, indicated how far into the community the desire to serve the youthful newcomers had reached.

For weeks in advance of their arrival the reception committee in Montreal was busy planning a warm yet discreet welcome for the young immigrants. Volunteer escorts were assigned to every automobile to make the youngsters feel at home from the moment they stepped off the train. But while this group was planning a subdued welcome, the home-finding committee was bombarding the public with news of the impending arrival. The publicity was calculated to yield the greatest number of homes possible, and it invariably featured the emotionally charged reminder that these were the children of six million martyred fellow Jews of Europe. As the day of arrival drew nearer these appeals became more and more intense, so that tremendous interest in the young newcomers was generated within the Jewish community.

Lappin writes that while co-ordinating committees were upset by the crowds that kept sweeping into the Centre, many of the youngsters relished the attention lavished on them. They were not merely objects of curiosity; they were the last link with European Jewry. And local teenagers also began to visit the Centre regularly. On many an evening these young Canadians would outnumber the residents; the largest number often being girls who had come "to flirt and look over the new boys in town." Instead of being a place of reception, the Centre began to take on the character of a neighbourhood community centre—often to the dismay of the staff trying to maintain some order.

Unlike the Toronto Centre, where finding a just solution to differing religious practices was a troublesome preoccupation, in Montreal one issue remained perpetually explosive—clothing. As Greta Fischer recalled, the war orphans had built up images of a dress code from Hollywood films and magazine advertisements which they had labelled the "American look." The first shopping trip was to be their big moment. However, prior to their arrival, the clothing committees, determined to acquire necessary clothing in the most economical way, had decided to establish clothing depots. The professional staff rose in opposition to this policy. They argued that the initiative required in choosing and buying clothes was the first step toward integration; and furthermore, they insisted that the youth were entitled to the same rights and opportunities as other teenagers in the community. Their argument that settled the matter in the end was the acknowledgement that clothing depots were too similar to the pauperized life they had known in the DP camps.

However, this solution produced confrontations of another kind. The American look could not be purchased within the given clothing allowance. The outcome of the dispute was often resolved by either the persuasiveness of the youngsters or the guilt-ridden vulnerability of the escort, most often a volunteer. To deny a survivor of the Holocaust a coveted piece of clothing felt like an act of downright cruelty. Back at the Centre outfits would be compared and charges of discrimination and favouritism would be levelled against the workers who were the ones held responsible for staying within the budget. It wasn't easy for them to learn to be thick-skinned to the accusations made by volunteers of their cold-heartedness and indifference to the needs of the children.

As for the smaller communities, in Ontario in particular, the impact made by the young immigrants is clearly conveyed in a letter by a community leader describing the reception of the first contingent of

European youngsters: "When we got off the train at Windsor there was no holding down the hundreds of people who had gathered to meet the kids. They took the kids shopping and when they ran out of community money, they dipped freely into their own pockets. It was an emotional binge that rocked the whole community."

CHAPTER SEVEN

Other People's Houses

THE LONG YEARS of political representation and manoeuvering which culminated in Privy Council Order 1647, the task of preparing Canadians, and finding eligible youngsters in the chaos of Europe were only the preliminaries. Yet to come was the long-planned final objective of making places for them in families, at school or work. None of it was easy. And embedded in that goal, taking many people unawares, was the filtering of images and expectations through the hard sieve of reality for both the newcomers and their Canadian benefactors.

Adding to the complexities, sea transportation was sporadic and unpredictable. One week an ocean liner would arrive at the docks in Halifax bringing twenty-five boys and girls from DP camps in Germany. A few weeks later another ship from Italy. At the end of the month perhaps another would dock with twenty-five children from Bremerhaven. A Congress memorandum of March 1948 gives some idea of the process.

> The International Refugee Organization succeeded in charting an extra boat. The *S.S. Nea Hellas* left Genoa March 10, 1948 and may be in Halifax on March 20. She carried 82 orphans from Italian camps. Forty are scheduled for the west, balance split between the central region and Montreal. The *Aquitania,* carrying 25 to 30, will leave Southampton on March 16 and should be in port on March 21 or 22. Half will go to

the Central region, the rest Montreal. Fifty from German camps due to leave Bremerhaven the end of March.

How, under these pressures, would it be possible to begin to find the right home for a youngster about whom one knew only that he or she had lost everything— parents and grandparents, shelter and safety, food and nurturing—and is left with only a story or, if lucky, one fading photograph of a family to bring to his new home? What constituted good parenting for these unknown orphans of differing ages and backgrounds? How and where were these surrogate parents to be found? And what could realistically be expected from parents already carrying their own family obligations?

The first step for Canadians was to revise their original expectations and accept that there would be "no little girls of five," as so many had requested when offering their homes, and accept older boys in their teens. The majority of orphans, they were told, would be between the ages of fifteen and eighteen, and only a small proportion would be girls. (Of the 1,123 who arrived, only 106 were under fourteen years and less than one-third were girls.) Even under the best conditions it is difficult to find homes for teenage children. How would Canadians, no matter how caring, deal with adolescents and young adults who had been dragged through more countries and experienced more brutality than even the most adventurous Canadian would likely to encounter, or even imagine, in a lifetime? And what bitter memories, dormant in the excitement of arriving in Canada, would later well up and challenge the peace and quiet of a Canadian home as the children struggled to adjust to a new country?

The pressure to find homes, as well as the terms of agreement with government, dissolved, or at least shrank, long-standing territorial disputes between agencies and people. There were misgivings when the Jewish Immigrant Aid Society (JIAS), the principal organization concerned with immigrant services for more than twenty-one years, was persuaded to sign over its role for the Orphans Project to

Congress. And approximately thirty organizations transcended their differences to join the search; psychologists, physicians, administrators, homemakers, and seasoned business people, likewise found ways to speak a common language in service to the greater goal. For no matter how well-designed the Project's blueprint, everyone knew that its overall worth rested on one goal—a good match between families and the children and adolescents. The merits of every preliminary step taken would be judged by this final act, so central to their future well-being. Yet little was known about them.

The only information people in Canada had to work with was the initial information from Europe which was hopeful. In February 1947 Congress received and distributed a report based on a six-month study entitled "Europe's Jewish Children Yearn for Love, Show Amazing Vitality to Build New Lives." Written by Dr. Paul Friedman, a distinguished New York psychiatrist, and the first specialist to survey the mental health of Europe's survivors, it had been commissioned by the American Joint Distribution Committee (AJDC) and carried enormous weight. It was quoted continuously. Although rather general in scope, it provided a basic description of the young people for whom substitute families were being sought. Written three months before permission was granted he stated: "I met and spoke with thousands of orphaned Jewish survivors who endured a decade of horror under Hitler. Their need for love and warmth, for sympathy and human understanding is tremendous, yet they show an amazing vitality and eagerness to build useful, happy lives."

Also included in the report were relevant excerpts from an interview Dr. Friedman had given at the New York offices of the AJDC on his return from Europe.

The Jewish boys and girls who lived through Nazism are not mentally sick. The brutalizing Nazi terror has left many of them shy, unemotional and withdrawn—a defense mechanism against the horror that was part of their daily lives; but those years have taught them also to be self-sufficient and to make the most of their opportunities. The ideal situation would of course be one in which every orphaned Jewish child could again find a home and affection. The children too feel an overwhelming need for a sense of identity, of family. [1]

A slightly more cautious but still positive report was received in a letter written by Amelia Igel, a child care consultant for AJDC in Paris on November 14, 1947, barely a month after the first group had landed in Halifax. She wrote that the group she accompanied to London, "seemed to be eager young people determined to work hard to build a new life in Canada. They are all children who have been deprived for so long of the normal give and take between adults and children, and have for so long had to depend on themselves to survive that they have little confidence in others and on the whole are very materially minded."[2] This jibes with what the Congress workers in Canada said; also some of the youngsters themselves, years later.

These were encouraging reports to Canadians given the images they had built up over the years of waiting. Yet they could go only so far in reducing fears about the young people they were being asked to take into their families. David Weiss, the newly appointed Executive Director of Jewish Family and Children Services in Montreal adopted a very cautious approach. An American social worker who had been asked to head the agency on the basis of his earlier work with refugee children in the U.S., warned potential foster parents of the kind of problems they could expect from the young survivors. To the chagrin of the community leaders who were scrambling to find homes, according to Toni Robinson, including her husband, one of the Project's leaders, Weiss and his well-meaning staff lost no opportunity in warning the community that because of their backgrounds many of the youngsters would experience nervous breakdowns. Weiss probably wanted to prepare people for the worst possible scenario, or as an experienced child welfare expert intended to counteract what he may have felt was the unrealistic optimism displayed by the leaders. He went so far as advising a gathering of the Jewish Junior Welfare League in November, 1947 that Canadian Jews should prepare themselves to be "mortgaged to pay for the upkeep of those who might have to spend the rest of their days in asylums and other protective institutions." Weiss also predicted that there would likely be a good number of delinquents among the orphans. In light of what was known about the basic components necessary for normal child development his comments were not surprising. One wonders what any group of todays' diagnosticians would predict after studying the histories of these young people.

Weiss was not alone in holding these beliefs. In the fifties, psychiatrists and psychologists tended to view almost all survivors of the Holocaust as dysfunctional people. The practice of affixing the negative label, "survivor syndrome"—the image of traumatized individuals who have difficulty coping with life in the present and will in the future—to all survivors stereotyped and stigmatized thousands of people and set them apart from "normal" people. It wasn't until well into the nineties that some social scientists became interested in studying the remarkable adaptive gifts of this group of people.

At the time of their arrival it was completely unknown whether the young survivors, given their traumas, could ever succeed in achieving mental stability. It is only in recent times that the study of the symptoms of victims of torture in Vietnam veterans and Southeast Asian refugees has led to an understanding of what has been identified as the post-traumatic stress disorder.

No one will deny that many of the war orphans exhibited strange behaviour when they arrived; but agency social workers soon began to understood this was not necessarily a sign of mental illness or crippling emotional disturbance— indeed there were very few needing referral to psychiatrists—but rather of unlearning techniques of coping with life in a brutal environment. There was no persuading the youngsters who were hoarding food in drawers and under matresses, for example, that they were in no danger of going without food again.

However, Weiss's views did not agree with the community to which he had just arrived, least of all with the staff of the agency; in the opinion of Ruth Tannenbaum, a social worker on the Project and later a faculty member of McGill School of Social Work, the difficulty was in the way he defined his role. "In an aggressive and opinionated manner he presented himself as an all-knowing therapist—the new panacea for human ills." This was in marked contrast to his highly regarded predecessor, Ginda Rosenblatt, a European trained physician and Canadian trained social worker. In Tannenbaum's experience, Weiss was responsible for creating "hard times for the staff because first and foremost, he was interested in gaining the favours of the board rather than promoting the needs of the social workers who were handling the most exacting responsibilities they had ever encountered." When the staff attempted to organize a union it provoked "a Red scare, and Weiss as handmaiden to the board searched desk drawers after hours looking for evidence of communist affiliation." Tempers reached such a boiling point that the staff mounted a campaign to get him fired, but failed. Greta Fischer also believed that Weiss' approach added to, rather than relieved, the pressures of an already over-taxed staff.

David Weiss died in 1992 so it is impossible to know why he began his job on such a pessimistic note and carried out his role as he did. Ironically, four months after the orphans arrived Weiss reported to the board: "It is interesting to note that many of the youth who are coming here are fairly well-adjusted and self-reliant. We have already handled 120 at this time."[3]

Prior to their arrival in Canada the child survivors were discussed and planned for as though they all belonged in one category. However, once they arrived in Canada, their diversity and the markedly varied experience of each one were immediately apparent. They came from fifteen European countries, 783 from concentration camps and 229 from hiding. Socially they were a diverse group. Some came from farming families, a sizeable number from comfortable middle-class families which had earned their livelihoods in business and small trades, and occasionally from a family of considerable wealth.

Celena Kolin's childhood story is one variation of "the hidden child" who arrived in Canada with the Congress Project. Celena came originally from the town of Sparacz in the Ukraine, on the Polish border. It was a small community with a magnificent castle at its centre belonging to a member of the Polish aristocracy. Parts of the estate were open to the public on special days and Celena loved to walk through its elaborate gardens hoping for a glimpse of the Duke's children out riding their horses. The other special event for Celena was Monday, market day. The peasants from the surrounding countryside, dressed in brightly coloured embroidered sheepskin-lined coats, would stream into town carrying their foods and wares. With them came the tinkling sounds of the tinsmiths at work. Celena loved to listen to the music made by the beat of the hammers as it filtered through the valley. It meant all was well.

Celena's father had been a professional soldier in the Polish cavalry before his marriage to her mother, after which he took over her mother's parents' store where they sold all kinds of coats. Celena spent a lot of time there, as she puts it, "watching my mother work at her beautiful roll-top desk. Mother was different from other mothers in Sparacz," she emphasized, "she was well-educated, bright, and emancipated. Her nails were manicured and she always smelled of perfume. She even smoked. And what made her stand out even more were the leopard coats she wore and the hats with attached veils that covered her face."

The family moved to Lvov in 1940 after the Russians invaded Eastern Poland. Two years later, when Celena was ten, the Germans set up part of the city as a ghetto and she saw them do terrible things. "Night after night we heard the screams of people being taken away and I thought I could never get rid of that sound going through my head. The streets became unsafe and children were warned they could be rounded up for the soap factories." When Celena caught rheumatic fever her mother decided to send her back to Sparacz for safety. But conditions there were bad and Celena and her aunt were forced to hide in an attic so small that they "had to lie down all day without even the chance to use the toilet or get food. But we could see the violence outside. Our house was ransacked many times while we hid, but the Germans never thought to look behind the armoire that hid the opening to the attic."

In the last letter Celena received from her mother she wrote: "Your garden is growing well." The handful of kasha seeds Celena had planted in the wet earth by removing an old brick had been her tiny garden in the ghetto of Lvov.

When conditions became more dangerous, and given her blonde hair and blue eyes, Celena's protectors risked sending her into hiding on a remote farm— but not before she was smeared with mud and given the name Marushka as a child of the mountain people, Gurame, orphaned by the floods of Zakopane. Celena spent the remaining war years in an isolated, primitive homestead cared for by childless Helga— long deserted by her husband—and gentle Frania who was both blind and deaf. She worked hard helping with the farm chores and was grateful for the food and protection.

However widely each child survivor's family culture and war experiences may have differed, they had one element in common. Each youngster had been separated pitilessly and suddenly from his or her family between the ages of five and thirteen. And most of those permitted to enter Canada had been sifted through a two- to six-month screening and observation process at the refugee camps which had facilities for children at Prien or Aglasterhausen in Germany. Apart from a thorough medical examination, they "were measured for their strength to have withstood those terrible shocks and their capacity to make their way in a new world" is how Celena interpreted what was behind her observation period at Aglasterhausen. Since no such system of calibration yet exists it is easy to speculate about how judgements were made when reading the anecdotal notes which Greta Fischer left among her personal papers.

> Manfred, age fourteen, is a German Jew, an only child of well-to-do parents. The father is known to be dead, the mother probably so. When one of the UNRRA team extended her hand to greet him, he shrank and then timidly took it. It was several days before he relaxed sufficiently to be able to join in the activities of the Centre. He was given as much special attention as circumstances permitted and has become one of the most popular of the youngsters. He laughs now, although in moments of repose one still sees the lines of strain on his face.

Most probably UNRRA staff based their assessments on intuitive judgements of observable coping behaviours or perhaps general affability. (My own experience on meeting many of the orphans during my research travels suggests what bright, talented and attractive children and adolescents most of them must have been.) The careful selection process rejected many who, for medical or other reasons, were considered unacceptable candidates for the Canadian Project.

Today, child psychology has accepted the theory of "resilience" to explain how some children manage to emerge from terrible experiences relatively intact, while others are broken or severely scarred. Larry Rotenberg, a child survivor in the Project who is now Director of Psychiatry at Pennsylvania's Reading Medical Center, fits this theory as though he were made for it. In Rotenberg's assessment, his survival as a whole, healthy personality is directly traceable to his early childhood:

> The richness of my early life, its predictability, its mosaic-like fabric of continuity and clear expectations, laid a foundation for faith in the universe which even the harshest

experience could not totally obliterate. For I remember as a little boy, even after the death of my parents, as I rummaged around the fields and forests of the Ukraine, that my sense that life was good and people were good. Another aspect... was my feeling of being special. I was the youngest, I was the one who was entrusted with many of the sacred religious duties in my family. I had become the great hope of the family. This expectation imbued me with a sense of specialness.[4]

Ben Lappin, agrees with Rotenberg's theory. In the progress report of his study of the war orphans Lappin noted that the records of the early childhoods of the war orphans indicate that the majority had known a happy family life and carried memories of warm, affectionate, close family ties.

> No matter how young they were when their families disintegrated, they all clung to recollections, some of them diffused and fragmentary, some of them coherent, but all of them powerful, of parents, of sisters and brothers; there are vivid descriptions of holiday celebrations, of synagogue services, of daily observances and the like.[5]

Likewise, Deborah Dwork writes: "As the two generations moved through the system of destruction the family structure was shattered, the last vestiges of pre-war parental power and authority were lost, but love and affection endured."[6] Dwork further notes that for those Jewish children who were old enough to remember, the memory alone of family life was a source of strength and solace. Similar sentiments were expressed by me. Throughout the war the child survivors sustained the hope or dream that some day the family would be reunited. In a vague way, they presumed that when the war was over their former life would be restored, and it was this conviction that brought them a certain inner stability.

Many of the youngsters picked up a number of languages as a part of their survival equipment, and in this Rotenberg also fits the mold. By the time he arrived in Canada as a teenager, he spoke nine languages, he says, quite fluently. Rotenberg also developed what he called "a chameleon-like quality which allowed him to fit in wherever and whatever way was necessary," with an uncanny ability to find somebody who would care for him. Whether in the fields of the Ukraine or in the orphanages of Western Europe, the few photographs he has of those early years always show him in the centre of the group, near its leader. He believes it allowed him to elicit interest from the people who had power over his life, which, he says, was not done in a calculated manner. Rather, he thinks, it emanated from an unconscious wish to be cared for and an ability to get the kind of attention which would make that possible. Once in Canada, he was able to find warm and caring parent surrogates for whom he became something of an adopted child without ever actually being formally adopted.

The way in which Joseph Gruber became a member of the Cohen family of Nova Scotia is another version of an adolescent who looked for a powerful protector. Nina Fried Cohen of Sidney was a widely respected community leader, as first Canadian Hadassah-WIZO Regional Chairman for Nova Scotia and Newfoundland, and later National President. Hadassah is the largest Jewish women's philanthropic and service organization in the country. Her account of how Joseph and Sigmund Gruber came to live with her family is a part of her memoirs.[7]

> While visiting Halifax from Cape Breton the winter of 1947 I learned that a group of war orphans from a concentration camp in Germany had just embarked from a ship there. The Halifax community provided entertainment for the children who were awaiting a boat-train for Montreal. I chatted with the boys and girls whose ages ranged from eight to eighteen. The scars of their human tragedy were painfully apparent—

huge eyes filled with despair staring suspiciously from pale faces. During the war I had often expressed the hope—if only we could save one child. Here was the opportunity. Canadian Jewish Congress intended to place some of the group in Cape Breton, and I was commissioned to make arrangements for fourteen children.

I was reluctant to choose our new son from the data submitted in advance, as I was responsible for the placement. I decided to await their arrival. On the appointed day I arrived at the dock in Halifax, excited and happy at the prospect of a foster son. When the children disembarked and massed in the shed, I turned to the escort and interpreter and said, "Please tell the children (most of them spoke Polish) that I would like to adopt a boy, any boy, and I shall choose him by recognizing the first hand I see raised."

Slightly to my right I saw a hand bobbing up and down in great excitement. Thus it was decided. Here was my boy. I hadn't even seen his face. The children made an aisle to let me through and a handsome blond, blue-eyed boy of fifteen came towards us. Curious to learn why he seemed so eager to come home with us, I asked the question. Joseph replied, "I noticed that you seemed to be in charge and I wanted to go home with the boss."

Nina Cohen told Joseph about her family and son Stuart, and he told them about his older brother somewhere in France who had also survived. Two weeks later, Sigmund, fourteen months older than Joseph, came to live with the Cohens. The memoir ends with these words: "Joseph's and Sigmund's adjustment was a two-way highway; we travelled together, always keeping in mind our ultimate destination. The journey was a challenge, and a happy, rewarding sojourn."

Struggles of a different order were experienced by some host Canadian families. For example, the professional social workers were expected to evaluate foster parents' suitability and this at times caused resentments to run high. Toni Robinson, wife of Benjamin Robinson, who was recently publicly honoured for her sixty years of dedicated community service tells this story.

My husband felt that as one of the principal planners of the Orphans Project it was incumbent on us to open our home both on principle and by way of setting an example. I had no objection. My children were grown by then, and we certainly could provide a young person with many opportunities as well as the privilege of going to university.

When the social worker came to evaluate us—and you must remember we were very prominent members of the community—she asked us stupid and outrageous questions: Is our home a happy one? Are my husband and I happily married?

Anyway, I had decided to take a young man—my husband left it to me— because there would be less responsibility. I had already brought up three children and wasn't anxious to go through it again. But when I met Roberta, who in answer to the question of what her ambition was, answered a "gebildiner mentsch" (a cultured, educated person), I was attracted to her immediately.

In the end Roberta came to live with us, but only after a struggle with the social worker. They had someone else in mind for us and they wanted to run the whole show. I never forgave them. We were very happy with Roberta and she with us. After earning a Ph.D. she has become a university professor.

Needless to say, things weren't always so rosy. Despite the best of intentions, painful troubles were never far away. A social worker's report in Congress' Ontario Archives gives a picture of the kinds of problems that arose.

Nathan is placed with the S.'s who live in an attractive five room, private home in a residential area. Nathan will share a double decker bed with Robert, aged nine. The S.'s lost a son who would have been the same age as Nathan had he lived. They spoke of desiring a close tie with Nathan; in effect they seem to want to replace their son.

During the initial period of placement Nathan seemed to to relate well to the S. family and they in turn spoke highly of him. However, as time wore on the S.'s began to express feelings about Nathan's failure to communicate with them and to relate on the close level they desired. Instead, he was aloof, did not share his problems, and played the role of the boarder rather than the child of the family. (In fact Nathan was concerned and preoccupied with his inability to obtain employment and his inability to continue his education.)

The S.'s decided that this was not what they wanted and asked that Nathan be replaced. He was distressed and embittered to learn of their desire to have him leave and found it difficult to contemplate another experience in a family home. However, he accepted placement with Dr. M., her husband, and young daughters. Everything went so well that in time the M.'s became interested in Nathan to the point that they offered him the opportunity to continue his schooling.

It was not unusual for many of the young refugees to make several moves before permanent settlement became possible. Lappin reports in *The Redeemed Children* that of the 137 war orphans who settled in Winnipeg, 92 required more than one home placement, and 28 more than four homes before permanent placement was possible. Virtually every activity the refugee children and adolescents undertook, according to Lappin, was filled with anxiety, none more so than when about to be received in a Canadian family. To each home placement they brought the hope that their days of wandering and rootlessness were finally at an end; but each placement was fraught with overwhelming difficulties.

As the youngsters moved from family to family, the agency became their "home base" to which they turned feeling rejected, bitter, and afraid to take the plunge again. Often they would first condemn the families who had disappointed them, followed by blaming the workers for not arousing the family's sympathy on their behalf, and ending up frequently questioning their own failure in adjusting.

Paradoxically, the very strengths that both war orphans and foster family brought to the relationship were often the basis of incompatibility. Many parents tended to approach the orphans with the same kind of firm supervision they used on their own children, striving to instill their middle-class values of good manners, respect for authority, poise and cleanliness. Furthermore, in those post-war years family protection began to be extended into early adulthood as a way of encouraging offspring to aspire to professional status and economic security. After what they had been through these controls and restrictions made no sense to the war orphans. They had become used to the kind of life which required open space, the ability to get away, to move quickly and to outwit. Survival under the Nazis depended on one's ability to evade control and avoid emotional attachment. To depend on anyone but oneself was often a quick road to death. Yet for their part, the European children, dreaming of a new life in Canada, may have visualized just such warm families, and many were desperately anxious to become part of a family again and put behind them the kind of existence they had known. But they were not prepared for the firm control and supervision that Canadian parents associated with good parenting. The tight parental supervision evoked bitter memories and suspicion. Authority for them was equated with tramping jack boots and the murder of their parents. They had survived, many felt convinced, because of their dexterity in fighting against that authority.

Thus the twin-edged dilemma: it was impossible for many of these adolescents to live harmoniously with adults, no matter how well-meaning, who saw youth and apprenticeship as synonymous; many parents on the other hand, could not relate to foster children other than as learners and dependents.

Equally crucial, as Barbara Stein (not her real name), now a mother and grandmother living in Montreal, articulated it: "As eager as I was to become part of a family again, I was afraid that by growing attached to a new set of parents, I would forget my own."

As one would expect, matching young newcomers to available homes produced a wide spectrum of good and unhappy fits. Moniek Lewkowitz, a successful businessman in Toronto, exudes gratitude when he recounts how his life began in Canada. "Congress really looked after us—they did the utmost for us. I can tell you it was a tremendous feeling to be put in a home and be given food and clothes. If you had a roof over your head and enough to eat and were free, you felt you could accomplish anything." As he speaks Lewkowitz searches for signs that I understand what he is saying. He is not sure. He tries another way. "It was a wonderful feeling to be put into a nice home with good people. We were so grateful to be alive and to have enough to eat that it drowned out our mourning for our families. That came later when things were normalized and we were less self-absorbed."

David Ehrlich was another of the fortunate ones. Now a cheerful, quiet-spoken Vancouver businessman, he recalls how he and the late John Hirsch, his Hungarian buddy from the refugee camp who became an internationally-recognized theatre director, were in the first group to come to Canada.

He and John, like so many of the others, had chosen to come to Canada knowing nothing about the country other than that it sounded like a good place to make a living. They chose Canada rather than the U.S. because their image of the Americans was either Chicago gangsters or fairyland Hollywooders. Winnipeg was promising to them because they saw on a map that it was located in the middle of the continent. That seemed like a safe bet from which to hedge their options if things didn't work out. And as it turned out, things worked

John Hirsch and David Ehrlich on Polson Avenue,
Winnipeg, July 1947
Courtesy of David Ehrlich

out extremely well for David and John, for Congress sent them to live with Alexander and Pauline Shack, and their daughters Sybil and Freda.

This is the way assignments were made: When a youngster had successfully passed a period of observation and the required certifications had been completed he was assigned to a group of 25 to 40 awaiting transportation to Canada. From the day he joined the group until the time he arrived in Halifax he remained in the care of an escort appointed by Congress. David and John's group was accompanied by Abraham Ram, a Montreal teacher. The escort became the young person's first contact with Canada, and so they would ply him with endless questions. For his part, the escort passed on to Montreal headquarters everything he could learn about the young person's backgrounds, education, religious observance and any preference he might have. Whenever possible, arrangements were made in accordance with requests and the details worked out were then conveyed to the escort and on to the youngster. A typical memo reads: "Gerta has a cousin settled in Galt. Would prefer being sent to her, otherwise she requests being kept together with her good friends, the G. brothers." Another says, "Elias with no friends or relatives will go anywhere."[8]

"Whenever possible" was a goal not easily reached in this Project which someone aptly called "one big master-stroke of improvisation from start to finish." Just twelve days before the first group was expected in Montreal the original plan of placing the orphans in private homes as soon as they arrived was abandoned in favour of a centre where they could be studied individually and given guidance and orientation before placement.

And with groups of 20 to 25 youngsters scheduled to arrive in quick succession on September 13, October 1, October 20, and November 8, it is understandable that Dora Wilensky, the executive director of Toronto's Jewish Family and Child Service wrote the following anxious letter to Congress Headquarters in December 1947:

We are concerned with the information that you are planning to send us between 35 and 40 youngsters since we are not confident that we can place 28 from the centre before that group arrives; moreover, 32 is all we can accommodate in the centre.

Given the many unknowns, fifty years later, Ehrlich has nothing but gratitude and affection for the Shacks, particularly Pauline Shack whom he remembers as a person who loved to feed and take care of not only people but birds and animals as well. "I am convinced," he says, visibly moved by her memory, "that when we later moved into a new house at the other end of the city, the birds she had fed in her garden, found a way in no time, to follow her to her new home." And during the war years, Mrs. Shack had kept a virtual open house for young men who came to Winnipeg as part of the Commonwealth Air Training Plan. Hundreds came at one time or another to the Shacks' home for a meal, and many stayed for a night or two in the spare bedroom.

Daughter Sybil Shack, a distinguished Canadian educator and author, now retired, continues to live in the house in Winnipeg that David and John once shared with her and her parents. The brick bungalow with grey cedar siding overlooks the Red River. Its front room is so filled with the late Mrs. Shack's robust plants that looking through the wide front bay window is somewhat like peering through a thick forest. Sybil Shack remembers clearly the events of early October 1947 that preceded the arrival of "our two orphans of the storm" in Winnipeg.

The telephone call was urgent. A group of orphans, survivors of the Holocaust, had landed in Halifax. Several of them were already on the train for Winnipeg, and not enough homes had yet been found to take them in. Would my parents consider taking a child? If not on a permanent basis, could they take one for at least a couple of weeks, until a permanent home could be found? My mother consulted with my father and me, but none of us had any trouble making up our minds. First, there was a precedent in the family. Following the Great War of 1914-1918, my mother's brother and his wife had adopted a war orphan, a young boy. Later, in 1938, when there seemed a possibility of Hitler allowing some Jewish children to leave Germany, my mother and father had indicated to Canadian Jewish Congress that they would like to adopt a little girl. However, no children were able to come to Canada at that time. It was a pity because by that time, although I was still living at home, my sister and I both teaching, there was both room and love waiting for an orphaned little girl.

A long-term commitment did not seem feasible. Mrs. Shack had barely recovered from a long illness, and Mr. Shack, who had worked for many years at Winnipeg Hydro, was only a few months from retirement on a small pension. Only Mrs. Shack's good management had made it possible to send two daughters to university, and to pay off the mortgage on their home. Still, the Shacks felt that since the house did have an empty bedroom, and the need was obviously great, they could cope for two weeks. So the answer was yes, they would be glad to welcome a little girl until adoptive parents could be found for her.

This story reveals Congress' state of organization. Even at this late date Congress wasn't sure who the children were. Many times, just as the deadline for boarding ship drew close there would be an abrupt change of travel plans. Since the war orphans held visas which did not have a time limit, they frequently had to give up their places to adult immigrants whose passports were at the point of expiry. A community would be alerted to expect a group on a certain date but at the point of embarkation, for various reasons, they would be bumped. Committees which had prepared receptions and home placements would be confronted at the last minute with news of change. On other occasions, reception committees spent futile hours at railway stations waiting in vain, finally to return home only to be called by baffled station officials and told that a group of boys and girls had unexpectedly arrived and were eager to meet their hosts.

Sybil remembers the day a social worker arrived, assessed the house and room, and went away satisfied, only to call a day or two later to say there were no little girls among the group arriving in Winnipeg. There were only boys:

Fine, we said. We would manage. Then another call. The boys were not little; they were in their late teens. Okay, we said, maybe that's even better. Our wartime guests had been mostly young men in their teens or early twenties. We were used to teenaged boys. We would manage. A day or two before our teenager was to arrive, a pair of social workers rang our doorbell. They were desperate to place the children who were due in shortly and the bed in the spare bedroom was a double bed. Could we possibly take two boys, for a very short period? Since on more than one occasion two boys had shared the bed in the small room for short periods of time, and since according to the social workers the situation was desperate, once more we said, yes, we would try. We would manage.

My father and I picked up the two boys and brought them to our North Winnipeg home. They were as unlike in appearance as we later discovered them to be in temperament. David Ehrlich was a handsome young man, blond and well-built, with the tatooed number of Auschwitz on his right arm. He was Romanian and spoke Yiddish, German, Romanian, and Hungarian. He also had a good working knowledge of French, having spent a few months in an orphanage in France while waiting for transportation to wherever. John Hirsch resembled a marionette on strings, tall and bony, with long arms and legs dangling from too short sleeves and trousers. His black hair sprang up from his head in wiry curls. He was very Hungarian, moving, dancing, jumping. He knew a good bit of German, no Yiddish, and only the few socially unacceptable English words he had picked up during his wanderings around Europe and months in an UNRRA camp. John was seventeen, and David "twenty-one." [David was one of the boys who succeeded in passing as an eighteen-year-old.]

Sybil can't remember just how the two weeks extended into a lifetime, but they did; not only to the immediate family but the extended family of aunts, uncles, and cousins unto the second and third generation.

In general, efforts to place the children in compatible homes could only be, at best, a haphazard process. The hurried way in which the Shacks became foster parents was not unusual. With some families and youngsters it was possible to identify salient features and make a likely fit. But most often simply finding a family—any family—was the paramount priority. Even if there were enough families there was no way a prospective home could be evaluated for the individual needs of a particular child while he or she was still in Europe. Once they arrived in town they were brought together with their foster families, within hours. At times the results proved unfortunate.

Celena Kolin, whose wartime story was told earlier, recalls arriving in Regina with no idea what was waiting for her except that a family would pick her up at the station. She was prepared for a positive experience, she remembers, because she had heard that the smaller the city the better the young refugees were treated. Her first impression seemed to bear this out:

Our train arrived in frozen Regina in early February, 1948. The train station was once again filled with warm-faced, enthusiastic people who whisked us off by car to one of their beautiful homes. The breakfast feast spread before us had an array of home-made delicacies that reminded me of what I had once known. When we could swallow not a mouthful more we were driven to Sam and Dorothy Promislow's dry goods warehouse. With the same warmth with which we were served food we were invited to take one of anything we wanted. I selected a sweater, a skirt and slip, and on the way out Mr. Promislow who was standing at the door making sure that no one left without some article of clothing insisted that I not leave without some lipstick and perfume too.

This first day in Regina was momentous and Celena was filled with optimism. By the second day it had evaporated.

I was assigned to a family who was totally incapable of understanding me. These complete strangers insisted that I call them mother and father from almost the moment I stepped inside their front door, and forced me to burn the one possession that I prized—my gorgeous new red dress, my first since the start of the war, given to me by the Red Cross in Germany. I suppose they had a fear of lice. I was used to that—in Europe after the war being de-loused was an everyday event. But what was unbearable, was their curling my straight hair, a feature I considered part of my personality, and the only one that I actually liked, unlike my accent and everything else about me. And to make matters worse I shared a bedroom with their grossly overweight daughter of my own age, who was likely the reason why I was placed in their home in the first place. She was ingenious in ways of never letting me forget that she wished I didn't exist. Compounding the problem, my love for learning and my early success compared to her poor school marks made me an easy target for her repeated rages. I was also used as cheap labour. Strange as it may sound, I wished I was back in the war because then I was treated as someone who had rights and feelings by the people who had sheltered me.

Filled with anger, Celena ran away and headed downtown saying to herself; "If Hitler didn't get me, then *they* won't." There was only one place for her to go and that was Congress' office where she found Tess Lexier, the social worker. Like social workers across the country, Lexier could only approach the adolescents in her care with knowledge of the deprivation, neglect and cruelty Canadian children had encountered; when she read the case records filled with accounts of the horrors these children had known she was shaken to the core and unsure where to begin to help. What she and the others were quick to learn was that many of the children were continuing to respond in terms of the environment they had left behind and needed a special kind of understanding.

Lexier listened attentively to Celena and prepared a cot in her living room for her to sleep on. (In standard social work circles this would have been censored as over-identification, or over-involvement with the client.) Two weeks later Celena was told a bedroom was being painted for her in the home of Ethel and Eddy Bassin whose elderly mother had just died. The Bassin home was everything the other was not, and Celena was received with warmth and kindness. Inevitably, some adjustment was required on both sides.

Ethel Bassin spoke of Celena as a beautiful and very bright girl who fit into the family immediately. "She was like a sponge she learned so quickly. Co-operative, and hard-working, she never needed to be told anything twice. She was also very 'structured.'"

Celena is incredulous that Auntie Ethel could be so tolerant and make these complimentary remarks about the compulsive, fearful Celena who arrived in the Bassin home, who did *everything* compulsively and to excess—no matter how it affected or disrupted the family. She admits no one could moderate her behaviour. "I over-did things, everything," Celena supposes, "because I was still afraid

that if I didn't do things absolutely perfectly I would be asked to leave."
Celena expands further:

> I realized that it was not only me who was bewildered. They
> were at no less a loss in knowing what to do with me, and I
> knew I must help them. A meeting of the ways was needed.
> Their sensitive, loving support gave me hope. Auntie Ethel
> and Uncle Eddie encouraged my return to school and praised
> me for the high marks I soon received. They knew almost by
> instinct what I needed and were always aware of what was
> upsetting. And in their wisdom they always treated me as
> someone who had her own point of view—and they never
> stopped reminding me to have a good time. In a way that I
> will never be able to understand, they knew how to restore a
> framework for normalcy within well-outlined limits. The
> Bassins were the most perfect people I have ever known and
> everything they gave me was positive, totally positive. I don't
> know how it was possible, but they never, ever hurt my
> feelings.

For some, like twelve-year-old Mariette Rozen, just learning to live
with a family posed insurmountable problems. Five years old when
she was first separated from her family in Belgium and sent into hiding,
she was moved from place to place so often and with so little advance
warning that she does not know how many families protected her. It
was all a blur. At the age of twelve when she arrived in Vancouver, she
was sent to live with a childless couple. Now a vigorous wife, mother
and grandmother who devotes herself tirelessly to a wide range of
community projects, Mariette remembers her reception as an initially
uncomfortable one:

> Mr. Satanov came to the station alone to meet me and take
> me home. When I entered the house Mrs. Satanov was ironing

in the kitchen with her back turned and she didn't move around to face me when I entered the room. It was clear to me that she didn't want me and that my presence in their house was Mr. Satanov's idea entirely. Mrs. Satanov and I did not speak one word to one another for three whole months, and in any case I couldn't understand her highbrow Polish Yiddish. She must have been convinced that I was some kind of thief because she would leave precious objects, like pieces of her gold jewellery in full display and look surprised when it was left there untouched. Since Mrs. Satanov wanted nothing to do with me, Mr. Satanov had to take all the responsibility for my care, no easy task. I had not lived in any routine since I was five and I was wild. My sullen expression said it all: 'You can't tell me what to do. I've lived on the streets until now and have no fear of being alone.' I ran away twelve times in the first year and each time Mr. Satanov found me he would say; 'You're mine, and you'll always be mine. I will find you wherever you go.' And whatever antipathy Mrs. Satanov may have felt toward me initially, it wasn't long before we grew to like one another. I marvel at how the Satanovs put up with me.

Mariette took a long time to learn to trust the Satanovs and to know what they meant to her. She lived with them until she married at nineteen and until their death thirty years later she considered them her loving family. All the community work she has been engaged in over the years is her way of repaying Mr. and Mrs. Satanov for their remarkable generosity.

When Canadian parents were first called upon to open their homes to child survivors, the photographs they had seen of concentration camps led them to expect docile, exhausted victims who would passively and gratefully accept their attentions. In every group there were always one or two with downcast eyes whose grief had silenced their voices and frozen their faces. To everyone's astonishment most ships brought aggressive, demanding teenagers, hardened veterans of concentration camps or lives-in-hiding who had had to meet a hundred challenges every day if life was to be sustained for another twenty-four hours. Foster parents were soon to discover that most of the children had emerged from years of degradation under the Nazis with a fierce dignity and pride in themselves and their Jewish heritage. It soon became apparent that many arrived in Canada with such a strong sense of personal worth and keen sensitivity for the principles of social justice that they judged Canadians accordingly and often found them wanting. Their sense of outrage had not yet spent itself, and nothing that was done for them ever seemed enough.

Many well-intentioned people were at a loss when faced with this kind of behaviour, and things were even worse when the host family was inappropriate for a placement. Such was the experience of Leah Kaufman, who now lives in Montreal with her family and has found her true calling as a Jewish studies teacher. Nine years old when she lost her family, Leah had run from place to place in the Ukraine during the war. At liberation when she was twelve, she was placed in an orphanage in Bucharest where she was over-worked and ill-treated. When she heard that UNRRA was good to children she made her way to a refugee camp in Salzberg and was persuaded by UNRRA personnel to apply to enter Canada under the War Orphans Project. Knowing nothing about Canada, and having nowhere else to go, Leah found the promise made to her irresistible. In Canada she would be able to become part of a family, go to school and lead a normal life. Leah had complete trust in the UNRRA staff. "They were like parents," she remembers. "They seemed to know unconsciously what we needed. And just like parents they supervised us well and were totally dedicated to us day and night."

However, events took a bad turn from the very start. The ocean crossing was rough and Leah perceived the other passengers aboard the SS *Sturgess* as aggressive anti-semites. The ship docked in foggy,

War orphans–Montreal group–and Joe Kage (left, bottom)
outside their reception centre, the former Herzl Clinic
(4650 Jeanne-Mance near Mont-Royal), 1948.
Canadian Jewish Congress National Archives

grey Halifax on Feb. 14, 1948 after what felt like an interminable crossing. Leah's judgemental attitude toward Canadians reflects what a number of the other young people also experienced.

> Loads of people came to look at us, and I felt like a monkey in the zoo with no one paying a bit of attention to our individual needs or what we thought. We were soon put on a train for the West and we began to pay attention to what people were wearing. We were very surprised to see that girls wore crinolines with big, long skirts. We concluded from this that there were no young people in Canada and that was why they were bringing us. In Bucharest girls wore short skirts.

As the train made its way westward some of the children got off at different points and by the time the train reached Calgary there were only two left.

> It was late at night and again a lot of people came to the station to stare at us. I was sent to live with a family that had three sons ranging in age from nine to twenty-one, and wanted a daughter. It was the wrong family for me and had I stayed with them I would have been destroyed. They didn't know how to show love to their own children, let alone me, and I found everything about them and the people they associated with cold, stingy and materialistic. They did nothing to help me unburden myself, but instead over-burdened me with other people's clothes, clothes they wanted to be rid of.
>
> And there I was believing myself to be of good judgement and having sound values, and being treated as though I had to be taught how to use a knife and fork. I suppose they meant well, but didn't know better. Everyone around me seemed to treat me as though I came from a very low class of society, while I felt vastly superior to them and certainly more cultured.

Luckily, the principal of the Peretz School, Mr. Heilig, recognized her love of learning and took Leah under his wing spending many hours tutoring and guiding her. He advised her to take teacher training and arranged for her to study on a scholarship at The United Hebrew-Yiddish Teachers seminary on St. Urbain Street in Montreal. "There is no question," insists Leah, "he alone was responsible for my entering the noble profession of Hebrew-Yiddish teacher." Helped with $30 in her pocket, a gift from Mr. Heilig, she arrived in Montreal by train and once again, sadly, found herself in a painful situation. She obtained room and board with an illiterate couple who treated her badly. "Everything I did," she lamented, "was either criticized or mocked. I was scolded for using too much water or not being clean enough, of having too many books, of being too quiet or talking too much... They didn't know what to make of me."

For Leah, Congress was invisible and their help non-existent. "They could have meant so much," she says regretfully. "But I was blessed by having the seminary. It saved my life. I read and studied and became the teacher I had dreamed of becoming. I later earned an M.A. in Jewish studies."

What happened to Leah was precisely what Congress had hoped to avoid. Through the duration of the Project it made every effort to know where the young people were so as to oversee the different stages of their adjustment. But sometimes it proved impossible and some, like Leah, fell between the cracks. There was a great deal of movement from one city to another as they looked either for better jobs, or better living conditions, and it was impossible to keep track of their movements. Many of the young people didn't want to have to "report to Congress."

The Jewish Vocational Services of Toronto did a follow-up study in 1950. Press releases in all Yiddish and Anglo-Jewish newspapers in the country produced only two replies. A second effort targeted on former workers—professional and volunteer—led to 131 of the war orphans willing to answer a questionnaire. On that basis Lappin extrapolates that of the total group about 75 moved to the United Stares as soon as they could—either to join relatives or feeling they would have better opportunities there—and severed all contacts with Canada.

A bedeviling question for all foster families was deciding whether it was in the best interests of their new family to ask about their pasts. Some people could give no credence to the stories they were hearing. It was not possible, they believed, for children to have comprehended such happenings, and the children in turn felt devastated and rejected by not being believed. Other parents, if they had younger children at home, wanted to protect their own children from hearing about the atrocities and did not allow any discussion on the subject. It wasn't until forty-five years later that Betty Cohen's (a fictitious name at her request) foster parents could allow themselves to hear that as a young girl she had spent three years in Auschwitz, a callousness that Betty finds unforgivable. "They were good people and as well-meaning as they were capable of being," Betty said, "but without knowing this they knew nothing about me." For Betty this blank is a metaphor for the alienating relationship she had with them, and she moved out as soon as she was able to support herself. Fortunately, she found the solace and warmth she needed among her fellow survivors and they "became the family we needed to one another. I don't know what would have happened to me without them," she adds. Betty later married a fellow Auschwitz survivor and they raised a family together.

Ernie Green, a Winnipeg businessman, is still stunned when he remembers the crude strategy used to silence him when he began to talk about his past: "I talked about starvation, lost relatives, and told stories about months in slave labour and the underground. My hosts told about *their* wartime hardships—sugar and fuel rationing, and washing machines being idle for lack of parts."

All the young Jewish children who lived through the Holocaust and survived were hidden and silenced children. Only those old enough to pass as adults or with bodies capable of adult labour were allowed to live. This must be understood in order to begin to imagine the profound silence and hidden self within each child survivor. And then later to be fed and welcomed by caring people who did not believe them sent that silent self deeper into its isolation. Some survivors have never broken that silence. Others, fortified by a life of productivity and accomplishment, and nourished by their family's love, are beginning to shed some of that inner hiding. All over the world, groups of "hidden children" are now forming to address the lifelong repercussions of living as a hidden child.

The Israeli author, Aharon Appelfeld, articulates the ineffable mental and emotional struggles endured by the war orphans who later arrived in Canada. Appelfeld was separated from his parents at the age of eight and sent to a concentration camp where his parents were killed. He escaped and spent the next three years in the forest, hiding out and struggling to survive, sometimes on his own and sometimes in the company of other fugitives. He writes that after liberation from a concentration camp at twelve, his "one desire was to sleep, to forget and to be reborn." At first he had a wish to talk incessantly about his experiences; this gave way to silence, but learning to be silent was not easy.

> For many years the members of my generation were concerned with the concealment and repression, or, to use a harsher word, the suppression of memory. It was impossible to live after the Holocaust except by silencing memory. Memory became your enemy. You worked constantly to blunt it, to divert it, and to numb it as one numbs pain. This battle lasted for years. People learned to live without memory the way one learns to live without a limb of one's body.[9]

But Appelfeld goes on to say that there was always someone who wanted to know what *really* happened and how he was saved, but "everything that happened was so gigantic, so inconceivable, that the witness even seemed like a fabricator to himself." The questions that came from the outside, he writes, were not helpful. "Those questions proceeded from an abyss of misunderstanding, from this world, and they were entirely unconnected with the world from which we came. As if you were to ask for information about hell or eternity. The feeling that your experience cannot be told, that no one can understand it, is perhaps one of the worst that was felt by the survivors after the war."

Many host families struggled endlessly to know how to address the orphan's past. Minny Loomer, originally from Regina but now a resident of Vancouver, had become Sylvia Ackerman's foster mother. Conscious of Sylvia's pain, Mrs. Loomer longed to help the child. (Sylvia married and moved to Toronto where she gave birth to twin sons. She died of cancer in her forties.) Deep down Mrs. Loomer felt that it would be good for Sylvia to talk about her past suffering. But Sylvia, a quiet, sad girl, became more silent and withdrawn with every attempt. Herbert Loomer, Sylvia's foster brother younger by two years and presently a Vancouver lawyer, speaks lovingly about the close relationship he knew with her. By one of life's mysterious coincidences, or designs, Loomer's daughter married Sylvia's son.

The Shack family was more successful than most, taking their cues from their "young guests, John and David." According to Sybil Shack:

> We learned not so much directly about their past experiences, of which they spoke little, but rather about their interests and personalities. We did not want to pry, to stir up what we knew were terrible memories, buts bits and pieces did inevitably emerge, not always through conversation. Sometimes through their indications of what they missed most in our cold prairie city—Oscar's delicatessen and Kelekis' chip stand that sold fries in paper bags for a nickel could not quite replace the beloved coffee houses of Budapest—and sometimes by their diversions and the company in which they found themselves most comfortable.

John was a doodler and initially his doodles consisted mostly of stick men hanging from lamp-post gallows. It took more than a year for the doodles to become designs of flowers, fruit and complicated abstractions. Then live faces appeared instead of corpses.

Sybil Shack also recalled how within weeks of their arrival Dr. Harry Stein, a professor at the Faculty of Education, University of Manitoba, did a psychological assessment of the newcomers. "David," he said, "is a bright young man, linguistically oriented, the more mature of your pair. But, Sybil, in John you have a genius on your hands." It had been obvious to the Shacks from the start that John Hirsch was "extraordinary." Dr. Stein's assessment merely confirmed their feelings.

Today the house of the Shack family seems filled with the presence of John Hirsch, who remained living there long after David Ehrlich had left to marry and start a family. The drawing John sent Ma Shack when he couldn't be there for her eightieth birthday is prominently displayed near the entry. Its colour is fading after twenty years of hanging in the sun, but its message of caring is still loud and clear. In the living room a place of honour is reserved for the carved cabinet that was once a prop in John's production of "Anastasia;" the water colour painting from a street stall in Bombay, rings for Sybil from Bangkok and Crete, pins from London, Jerusalem and Casablanca, and much more, blend into a truly exotic showcase. And watching over it all is the large white rooster from Venice which arrived complete with bills of lading in a crate too big to go through the door.

Sybil recalls that she could see no future in the theatre for the boy who wanted to design sets for the ballet; who, before his untimely death, received every honour Canada could give him, and had become a celebrity in the U.S. and Europe. She recites with the delight of someone who never tires of repeating it to a new listener the comment made to her one day in Stratford where she had gone to see one of John's productions. "A woman asked me how it was that I spoke unaccented English, while John who was obviously a much younger " brother, had such a noticeably foreign one.

Few family stories may have worked out as well as the Shacks did with David and John, but many did succeed in finding large measures of compatibility. Others were terrible, yet the children went on to healthy and productive lives.

CHAPTER EIGHT

Fitting In

POLICY SET BY CONGRESS, from the outset rested unequivocally on the promotion of independence and self-sufficiency. Each youngster was expected to go to work as soon as possible after arrival; only those few with demonstrable special talent would be able to resume their education, that is, if funds from private benefactors could be found. This was very disappointing to the many who had dreamed of continuing their education in Canada. There was no alternative, given the strain on resources, but in another sense it conveyed the message that each youngster was thought to be healthy and capable of determining his own life.

It was one thing for the orphans to be received by a warm and caring community who found homes for them, but quite another for the youngsters to face the inappropriateness of the skills they had acquired in refugee camps. This training had often been given to them by the Society for Rehabilitation and Training (ORT—abbreviation of three Russian words) an international Jewish organization which had been established shortly after liberation in or near DP camps. The young people displayed their tradesmanship with pride and a strong sense of mastery.

Unfortunately, there was little demand in the Canadian labour market for some of the skills they had learned in Europe. For example, quite a few boys came with some knowledge of diamond-cutting, but Canada offered few employment opportunities in this industry. Similarly, the group boasted a substantial number of dental technicians, another field that offered few job possibilities. It was true also for watch-making. The young immigrants, Lappin writes, would often react with shock when they discovered that their prized vocational skills had limited value in their new communities.[1] Lappin further notes that in spite of many difficulties most of these young men and women were able to carry to new jobs and occupations the same drive and motivation which had enabled them to survive the ghettos and concentration camps.

Working in their favour was the fact that the Canadian economy was booming at the time. Not only was there an abundance of jobs, but new apprentices like them presented no threat to experienced older workers. The period of post-war industrial expansion was an era in which learners were generally well received by the industry they chose to enter. This was especially so for the needle trades where so many war orphans found work, and perhaps was one of the key factors in the quick vocational adjustment of the group.

Although this adjustment was on the whole successful it was accompanied by a pervasive grievance about low wages which meant that after a week's work, many of them still had to go the family agency for supplements up to the $25 limit. Some charged they were being exploited, and in some instances the allegations were true. Another complaint often voiced by the young people was that they had been hoodwinked in Europe by people who promised them that the Canadian communities would make up to them for the misery they had endured under Hitler. They contended that they were promised university educations.[2] Unfortunately, immigration agents and agencies coping with hundreds of people trying to make up their minds would often describe Canada in glowing terms in an effort to end indecisiveness, as by both Lottie Levinson and Greta Fischer.

Moniek Lewkowitz's experiences in making his way in Canada are typical of the kind of enterprise many of the young survivors demonstrated. Lewkowitz had wanted work as an electrician for which he believed he possessed natural skills. However, the union was not admitting new members; instead he found work sewing caps in a factory. He worked there for about a year and when he was not given the five cent raise the unionized workers were given, he decided to leave and start his own headwear factory. He and a friend he had met on the ship to Canada bought two sewing machines and that is how they began their business, which later grew into an enterprise importing children's wear. Lewkowitz explains the source of his energy and ambition in this way:

> Everyone was determined to achieve something, to get somewhere. If we saw for example, that Joe had purchased a car from the profits he made peddling rags, we would think, 'if he can do it, why can't I?' It didn't matter one bit if it took working sixteen hours a day. Remember, we had been deprived of so many things for so many years that our whole life was centred around working and making something of ourselves. The drive to be somebody in life came from our good backgrounds. These beginnings led us to prove that we *could* make a *mentsch* (an honourable person) of ourselves in spite of it all. 99 percent of us became decent people.

Arnold Friedman, a successful Toronto businessman, recounts his efforts to fit in. He spoke with the quiet authority of someone not only accustomed to speaking his mind, but who quite enjoys having an audience. He is unabashedly proud of his luxurious house, which he himself designed, especially the enormous dining room "where there is always room at the table for everyone in the extended family and many guests as well." Unmistakably, family life dominates the Friedmans' life, as it does for so many of the survivors.

As she prepared tea, Mrs. Friedman with theatrical laughter exclaimed: "Arnold and I have known one another since we were children. I remember the exact moment I saw him for the first time. I was five years old and leaning against the brick wall watching the front entrance." She then jolts the listener by adding; "He had just stepped down from the transport that had brought him to the concentration camp, Theresienstadt. I had been taken there before him."

Arnold takes up the story from there, adding that they met again after the war at Prien, an UNRRA refugee camp.

Following liberation from Auschwitz I returned to my home in the Carpathian mountains only to find no sign of my family. My childhood home was occupied by strangers, but instead of welcoming me back they looked at me and asked, "Why did you come back?" I couldn't think of staying there any longer and with the borders closing headed quickly for Prague where I had heard children under sixteen were registering to go to an orphanage in England.

I managed to get to Prague in time to join a group being sent to Scotland where I was taught Hebrew, English and agriculture in preparation for going to Palestine. Two years later I was given the option of going to Canada.

When I arrived in Toronto I was sent to live with a family in Guelph and was able to attend school. Being the tallest and oldest student at school was one problem, but when my teacher would not believe that a Jewish boy could possibly have been born on a farm, although I was able to demonstrate that I knew more about cattle and farming than anybody else in the class, I was convinced it was time to return to Toronto and look for a job.

The first of many jobs I held was in the testing laboratory of a paper factory where I learned quickly and proved myself to be a diligent and ambitious worker. In every job that followed, much to my astonishment, I found myself being promoted at a faster pace than even my own ambitions.

Today Friedman is president and chief excutive officer of a number of successful business enterprises. He explains his success in this way:

> We had to become entrepreneurs because, unlike me, most of my fellow refugees were unable to even fill out a job application. All we had was our limited skills and muscle. It's true we did have that acquired skill that I call street smartness, but there is really no word for the strategies and tactics you develop to slip away from murderous situations that face you every moment of the day. For one thing I learned that it was always safer to be in front because then you could fall back; if in the back you have nowhere to go. I always made sure that I was in the first rows, and on numerous occasions that was what spared me.
>
> It was these kind of survival techniques which we then translated into entreprenurial undertakings, and we multiplied into a wave of enterpreneurs who created industry in this country that accepted us. And what that meant was hard work for limitless hours.
>
> You must also remember that in the concentration camps the Nazis permitted us to live only as long as we were able to work and produce for them. The fear that we brought with us compelled us to keep digging, to keep on working. The results are obvious. Many people who were totally illiterate became millionaires. They could not stop working because the fear they brought with them kept on driving them, kept the adrenalin going. Many of our people who today are in their 60s and 70s don't know how to stop. They have done wonders with the limited knowledge they had. Not one of us ended up on skid row. Each one of us has accounted for his life in spades.

Arnold is convinced that the source of his hardiness of spirit lies in realizing that having lost his family he had no one but himself to rely on.

As a fifteen year old caught up in the Holocaust he feels he was more of a bystander than a participant and seemed to have viewed his suffering not as a personal tragedy, but rather from a third party perspective. At fifteen, he says, "faced with a firing squad does not terrify you because it doesn't make sense, and I didn't try to analyze it. It was all too overpowering for tears."

On the other hand Allan Weiss chose to come to Canada simply as a waystation to the U.S. where he wished to join his brother. Since he had already crossed the whole of Europe without any permits, he assumed he would have no problem crossing to the United States, but he was refused entry. Once in Canada however, he never left because, as he says, "I met some beautiful people, the Montagnes, and became a member of their family."

Weiss had had some training as a jeweller and started out in that trade, but work soon became scarce and he had to look elsewhere. He found a job selling high quality aluminum windows, a new product on the Canadian market. He laughs as he remembers how poorly he spoke English and is still puzzled as he recalls how easily people bought his wares anyway when he went door-to-door. He was successful from the start. A short time later he set up his own business manufacturing windows, plastic parts for windows and other industrial purposes as well as thermal-pane windows.

While many of the orphans banded together and helped each other, Kitty Salsberg wanted nothing to do with her fellow Europeans after she arrived in Canada. Anything in any way connected with Europe was "to be avoided like the plague," she says. Her all-consuming goal was to become a bona fide Canadian in the shortest possible time.

In Europe she had been assured she would be given a family and she would accept nothing else. Remembering herself as a shy sixteen-year-old feeling very much the outsider, it amazes her to remember how assertive she was about insisting on getting a family. The Feingolds, a childless couple in their fifties, really wanted a younger girl, and she thinks that it was mostly Mr. Feingold's idea to accept her. He adored

That spare room in your home can fulfill a promise for David.

David does not need more than your own child

He has come a long way from war-torn Europe.

He needs a home, a room in your home.

David is among the first 1000 healthy, happy boys and girls who are being brought to Canada by the Canadian Jewish Congress. Their future in Canada, their happiness, their lives depend upon people such as you. They need someone to belong to — someone to love them — someone to want them.

David most likely will soon be working and will be able to pay his own way — but he needs a home — now!

David does not need more than your own child

Pamphlet, 1948. A green band was visible when closed (top).
There was additional text when opened (bottom).
Canadian Jewish Congress National Archives

Kitty and would buy her anything she wanted, even though he earned only a modest living in his neighbourhood grocery store.

To Kitty "Toronto felt like a big village full of boring cottages." Soon after moving into the Feingold's bungalow she was able to attend high school at Bloor Collegiate, and developed "a craving to own a bicycle which I recognized even at the time as being inappropriate for someone my age. But to me, riding a bicycle up and down the streets was tantamount to waving a Canadian flag. It made me feel like a wholesome Canadian and represented as well, a missed childhood.

"Regretfully Chake Feingold could make no sense of anything that mattered to me. She reminded me of my Aunt Gissy—critical and resentful by nature rather than intention. Originally from Kiev, Mrs. Feingold was unsympathetic to anything from another culture or a different way of doing things. For example, she was disturbed that I didn't know how to speak Yiddish and I can't help feeling that because of it, believe it or not, she saw me as a fraud, only pretending to be Jewish." However, over time differences were smoothed over and eventually the Feingolds became for Kitty the good and loving family she had longed for. She cherishes their memory.

The highlight of Kitty's first year in Canada occurred as a result of missing a school exam. She overslept, which was very unlike her. When her teacher phoned the house to see where she was she rode her bicycle at breakneck speed to school. Arriving late she wrote feverishly, convinced she had ruined all her chances to continue her studies, and hardly noticing that it seemed an unusual exam.

Kitty's black, expressive eyes sparkled all the more and the look of pride on her face was quite unmistakable as she said. "I scored the highest marks in the class..." She paused, glowing with pleasure at the happy memory and added, "that is, the highest marks for grade 11 when I was only in grade 9. I was a voracious reader which gave me a decided advantage. I was permitted to skip a grade and felt like a star, as you can well imagine."

Kitty loved school and decided to become a teacher. She applied to

Normal School and was told that in order to be accepted in the programme she would have to get rid of her accent by Christmas. The Feingolds also presented an obstacle—they didn't want her to attend university because it would make her too smart to marry. "No boy would want me, they told me and furthermore, if I persisted in heading in that direction I would have to leave their home. But nothing could stop me. I applied for a scholarship and when I was awarded one the Feingolds felt forced to relent. After all, it was unthinkable to expect me to give back the money granted me."

Kitty's career as a teacher has been most rewarding and she is now teaching English as a Second Language, which gives her great satisfaction.

The story of how Joseph Rothbart found a way to fit into Canadian society takes many turns. Fifty-two years after entering the country as a Congress-sponsored adolescent, Rothbart, the long-time Executive Director of Mount Sinai Sanitarium, re-located from Ste-Agathe to Montreal, is seated in a large office filled with the smells of fresh paint and new wood. The new building, designed and built as a specialized treatment centre for pulmonary diseases, was recently completed and is the realization of his dream. He walks along the colourful, wide hospital corridors pointing proudly to the latest equipment and conversing with fellow staff and patients with an affection that suggests this is his home and they his family.

Rothbart is a robust man well-satisfied with his lot in life who speaks forcefully in a strong but nuanced voice. The events he recounts, his manner of speech, the way he moves, the look on his face—give the impression that his personality has incorporated and harmonized many contrasting features: gentle and fierce, sad and playful, humble and aggressive, philosophic and pragmatic. And one dominant expression overrides all the rest—"to be alive is a colossal triumph."

Rothbart's credo of self-reliance—"you had to find the strength to save yourself"—is the mold that shaped his philosophy.

Soon after arriving at the Reception Centre in Montreal he was chosen by the Smith family to live with them. In many ways they were an ideal foster family. Rothbart described them as kind and generous people who lived in a well-furnished house on Terrebonne Avenue bordering on a beautiful field of trees and flowers. They offered him the opportunity to attend school. Yet he could not accept their generosity and he chose to leave their home because they wanted to adopt him and have him take their name. "At seventeen, I had to make my own decisions," he declares calmly.

Leaving the Smith home meant entering the world of factory work. Since Rothbart lacked language and special skills of any kind, the tasks given him consisted of sweeping and cleaning. No matter how hard he tried to make it through a working day, Joseph's willpower seemed to run out by the early afternoon, hours before he was entitled to a day's pay. With a grin and a flourish he recalls: "The first thing I would do when I left the manufacturing plant was to phone Greta Fischer, my social worker at the Centre, to tell her I had walked out. And she always had time to listen to me." He then lowers his voice and says quietly, "She was the only person I had to talk to. Often I created a problem in order to have a reason to go to see her."

Fischer's steadfast, continuing help was certainly a key factor in getting Rothbart through rough times. In a paper presented at the Canadian Conference on Social Work in Vancouver in 1950, Dora Wilensky, Director of Toronto's Jewish Family and Child Service, highlighted the significance of the dynamic relationship between the social worker and the young people from Europe: "It was the worker's consistent warmth and understanding, and the stability which she gave these children as the agency representative, that saw them through their initial feeling of failure, fear and distrust." Greta Fischer, as she is remembered by Rothbart, clearly fulfilled Wilensky's definition of what was needed when Wilensky wrote: "They needed help in accepting limitations, in recognizing the responsibility they carried for their own adjustment, in facing squarely the difference between real and imagined independence."

Rothbart continues: "The first thing Greta would ask was whether I had gotten paid. Of course I never had, and she would immediately set off for the factory either on foot or by streetcar requiring many transfers, to collect what she believed was my honestly-earned money." It was no accident that most of the factory owners were Jewish, and it didn't take much of an effort, according to Fischer, to remind them of their responsibilities to the young orphans, and persuade them to add some extra dollars as an expression of their humanity.

During the hours Joseph swept the multi-coloured pieces of discarded fabric into neat piles, he saw before him a multitude of possibilities, but no way to attain them. One day, he was unexpectedly summoned for another medical examination. In the doctor's waiting room he ran into one of the girls with whom he had crossed the Atlantic Ocean. Whispering, she impressed upon him the necessity of never admitting to having had any lung disease. Since Joseph had indeed suffered a bout of pneumonia in one of the concentration camps, he was grateful for this advice.

When questioned by the examining doctor about prior illnesses, Joseph denied having had any. What he didn't know at the time was that pneumonia leaves a spot on the lung, and given the diagnostic tools of the day, this was easily mistaken for T.B. He was sent immediately to Mt. Sinai Sanitarium in Ste. Agathe. Three months later was it discovered that a misdiagnosis had been made.

The fact that he was hospitalized some sixty miles north of Montreal in the heart of the Laurentian mountains was no deterrent to Fischer's visiting Joseph. She persuaded him to take a job in the sanitarium's storeroom rather than return to Montreal and his sweeping merry-go-round. Furthermore, she won the agreement of the registrar of Sir George Williams College in Montreal to accept him as a student. It was not in Fischer's nature to boast, and Joseph regrets that he never learned how she managed this.

What Fischer *had* made loud and clear was her objection to the inappropriate use of the newly-devised and widely-relied upon vocational testing tools to evaluate the European youth. It troubled her that these culture-tainted instruments were used with the young survivors, and she fought many battles on behalf of boys and girls whose gifts or interests did not tidily transpose onto a coded score sheet. Gathering and presenting her intuitive evidence with a force and certainty that could create doubt in the most diligent examiner, Fischer was a formidable opponent for the psychologists.

Joseph Rothbart was very busy. He worked Saturdays and Sundays to make up for lost time. He learned English from the resident occupational therapist in her free time in the evenings; and commuted the long distance to Sir George Williams. His efforts paid off. He was soon promoted to bookkeeper and after completing a degree in commerce he became assistant executive director, and then director, at the institution where he had once been wrongfully sent as a patient.

CHAPTER NINE

Looking Back

THE ADULT SURVIVORS of the Holocaust have now been studied extensively. Generally, investigators have assumed that the survivors are traumatized and impaired individuals. Although this may be true for a segment of the survivor population—there are unquestionably some seriously depressed and disturbed individuals among them— most adapted well after their agonizing experiences. The greater part of our present knowledge has been expressed in terms of pathology and therapy, both of which assume that the experience of the Holocaust has so permanently damaged the individual survivors that their reality is irrevocably filtered through a skewed view of the world. The years have proven otherwise. Although their sufferings marked them and they are "different," the vast majority have emerged as whole people, leading lives as normal—however that is measured—as the rest of us who have not experienced the horrors they lived through.

What has been neglected is a systematic attempt to understand the remarkable strength and adaptation with which they rebuilt their lives in strange environments, learning new languages, trades and profes- sions—despite the painful wounds. It is the survivors' resilience which is most striking—their ability to work productively and creatively, their capacity to build a family life, and their heightened appreciation of life. This is an extraordinary achievement, especially so for the young survivors.

Developmental theories generally suggest that the younger the individual at the time of trauma, the more severe and lasting its effects.

Congress Bulletin

VOLUME 4, NUMBER 9. | **MONTREAL, CANADA** | **SEPTEMBER 1947**

Failure Faces Orphans Movement Unless Homes are Found for Them

JIAS ASSISTS EVERY PHASE OF PROJECT

Joseph Kage, assistant to the National Executive Director of the Jewish Immigrant Aid Society of Canada, has been loaned by his organization to the orphaned youth movement which the Canadian Jewish Congress

Joseph Kage

is sponsoring from Europe. Mr. Kage, who as an experienced social worker has been on the staff of McGill University before coming to the JIAS, has been placed in charge of the reception center in Montreal, and supervises the group activities and the adjustment process of these youngsters before they are placed in foster homes. At the same time each of these young immigrants is attached to a trained social worker who assists in his personal problems together with the Big Brother or the Big Sister who will volunteer for this work.

Mr. Kage has also been associated with the Family Welfare Bureau of the Fed- (Continued on page 5)

The youngest member of the European refugee children to land on these shores is seen disembarking from a specially-chartered plane which brought them from Halifax to Montreal. Some older members of the party are following her.

Two Groups In Canada; Third Is Now En Route

The second group of war orphans arrived in the Dominion during the second Succoth week-end. They stayed over in Halifax for two days to avoid travelling on the festival and homes were arranged in the community for them by the local Congress committee and by the sisterhood of the Robie Street Synagogue. Noah Heinish, honorary vice-president of the Congress is supervising the arrangements. The sisterhood committee consists of Mesdames A. Newman, Charles Aron, R. Goldfarb, Julie Silverman and Nathan Rubin. (Continued on page 3)

JEWISH FOSTER HOMES URGENTLY NEEDED FOR ALL

The most serious difficulty facing the arrangements committee in charge of the movement of war orphans from Europe to this country is the shortage of foster homes in which these young people can be placed. Spokesmen of the committee are frank in stating that unless many more homes are immediately found for this project the entire movement may be jeopardized.

David Weiss, director of the Family and Child Welfare Bureau of the Federation of Jewish Philanthropies of Montreal, outlined for the Congress Bulletin the nature of the needs.

"The children coming are all in their teens; they are healthy, cheerful, well-bred youngsters, considerate and alert, and the social workers of the Jewish Child Welfare Bureau who are assisting in the project speak highly of the contribution that these youngsters can make to home life.

"We are looking for Jewish homes where these young people can find a place to sleep and to eat, perhaps where they can bring their friends or where they can find boys and girls for whom they would be (Continued on page 2)

Montreal Readers Please See Page 16

Congress Bulletin, September 1947.
Canadian Jewish Congress National Archives

Using this premise, one would predict that those who were child survivors were at greater risk throughout their lives than adult survivors. The young survivors who came to Canada as part of the War Orphans Project challenge this belief.

In each interview I held with the men and women who had been child survivors, now in their sixties or seventies, I was aware of their ongoing pain stemming from loss of parents and family, and from the horrible circumstances of their deaths. Their hunger for some link with the past through family, for their lost childhoods, and for the unrecoverable parts of themselves which they buried in their struggle to survive, shadows every moment. Yet in spite of these losses the most striking quality about this group of people is their affirmation of and deep appreciation for life. Robert Krell, Professor of Psychiatry at University of British Columbia and himself a child survivor from Holland, articulates his thoughts:

> We all face the challenge to live a meaningful life, but the survivor's awareness of death may inspire an even greater call to not live trivially. Therefore, in light of all that has happened to the survivor's family and people, there exists a potentially creative, dynamic force—derived from a horrendous past— to lead a socially constructive and self-healing life.[1]

Who in the 1940s would have imagined such positive outcomes? At that time there were high expectations that the application of newly-developed approaches based on pschoanalytic theory and ego psychology would bring new insights. There were similar expectations about new testing instruments that promised certainty about human behaviour, and, more than that, future potential. As is so often the case when exciting new theories are first formulated, especially theories that fill a long-standing void, they were applied with great enthusiasm and false confidence. Psychiatrists, psychologists, and social workers were keen to flex their newly-developed clinical muscle, and expanded their taxonomy to this group of highly distressed survivors. By the 1960s new categories such as "survivor syndrome" and "survivor family syndrome," were created, and having created them, the clinical community busied themselves fitting people within those definitions.

The research literature spelled out in ever more sophisticated ways the extent and patterns of the psychological and social maladaptation of the survivors. In the rush to document *what went wrong* no one seemed interested in learning *what went right*—how the survivors, adult and youth, found the inner strength to establish themselves in a world that did not, and could not, comprehend the tragic abyss from which they had emerged.

The extent of the damage these labels produced can never be known. What we do know is that many of the newcomers felt stigmatized and rejected for being "survivors." I interviewed a man I'll call Mike who since early childhood had been fascinated with the way mechanical things worked. All through the war he dreamed of a career in engineering. When he arrived in Montreal and found a job as a mechanic's helper, he quickly realized that his natural aptitude, despite his lack of training, gave him an advantage over the other workers. Yet it led him nowhere. "I was called a Holocaust survivor, a damaged person," he says philosophically, "how dare I consider enrolling in an engineering programme?" And he never did. Mike makes his living as a salesman.

At the other end of the spectrum is Robert Berger, presently living in Boston. He and John Hirsch had been buddies in a European refugee camp where they both applied to come to Canada as part of Congress' Project. Berger never understood why he was sent to the U.S. instead by the European child relief agency. Interviewed in his home in 1992 he spoke with the certainty of someone who has spent a great deal of thought looking back. The poignant way in which he spoke recalled the impression formed in talking with other survivors.

"I believed restitution equals loss and expected to be King of Berger Kingdom. I found instead an empire of Do-For-Yourself." Berger chose to become a heart surgeon, and was one of the first to perform coronary by-pass surgery. "Facing life and death in the operating room was like re-enacting life in the concentration camp, but with me being in control, most of the time."

A number of the men and women who told me stories about how they survived and made their way in Canada believe it was their age— that they were children and adolescents—which shielded them from understanding the nature of the evil they had experienced. This lack of comprehension enabled them to preserve some hope, they believe.

Joseph Rothbart, who was one of the first boys to arrive in Canada, endorsed this view after studying the mental landscapes of his generation of child survivors. In his sixties when interviewed, he maintained that "age is always the dividing line." When he was driven into a concentration camp at the age of thirteen he didn't really understand what was happening to him. "Had I been taken at sixteen I would have understood," he said, and is convinced it would have left a different mark. "Those who are two or three years older than me, I believe, are deeply scarred."

Unlike many post-war immigrants and refugees who came to their new country accepting the hard fact that the status they had had in their homeland could not be recovered, the war orphans who came to Canada made no such compromise with their new country. Despite the grimness of their experience in Europe they were, after all, teenagers, and many cherished teenagers' romantic dreams of glamorous careers. They were going to conquer the world and nothing was going to stop them. Allan Miller, one of the child survivors said: "I never lost the feeling that we won because we endured, that we were invincible. We were drunk with freedom. In some way that exhilaration never left us. It became a sort of permanent optimism."

One wonders how, after such savage formative years, these young people managed to build new lives without a deep disrespect for human laws and civil institutions. There is an almost complete absence of juvenile delinquency or crime among the young people or the adults.

William Helmreich, Professor of Sociology and Judaic Studies, CUNY Graduate Center, though acknowledging that these questions need to be researched further, states that "the fact that the survivors came to America during a period of relative prosperity and received a great deal of support from Jewish agencies, as well as from relatives and friends, was certainly very important." He further asserts, as do many other authors and survivors, that the Nazis were unable to destroy a basic value system that had been developed in families and communities prior to the war.[2]

Larry Rotenberg reflected on these themes in a personal essay. He was seven years old when the Germans forced his family to march into the Ukraine in mid-winter from their home in Romania. By the time he was eight Rotenberg had lost his parents and brother. He and his sisters managed to stay alive by feeding themselves on grass, acacia leaves, scraps of food when they could be found, and trading whatever could be found to keep body and soul together. Rotenberg was thirteen when he arrived in Canada in 1948 under the auspices of Congress.

Now in his sixties and a psychiatrist, he has asked himself many times: "Why am I not psychotic? Why am I less neurotic than I might have expected to be?" He further wonders how he was able to distance himself from the experience of the Holocaust "yet perhaps use it as a means toward achieving growth." In attempting to find some answer he readily admits that he possesses enough of the Holocaust survivor syndrome to make him feel that he has not been entirely free of injury caused by his experiences. "My sense of hyper-vigilance, my easy assumption of the worst possible outcome of a particular situation is a part of it." However Rotenberg attributes the reasons for having done so well, despite such enormous traumas in his early years, to his family. "The unequivocal warmth and affection which marked those early years," he writes, "were undoubtedly the most important in sustaining me through the bad times. The richness of my early life, its predictability, its mosaic-like fabric of continuity and clear expectations, laid a foundation for faith in the universe which even the harshest experience could not totally obliterate."[3]

Clearly, another factor was his capacity to learn quickly and become a good student. When Rotenberg arrived in Canada his burning desire as a thirteen-year-old boy was "to put as much distance as possible between myself and my past." He did this by throwing himself into becoming "more North American than others," adding that "to say that I overcompensated would be an understatement." When he graduated from high school he received the highest grades that year in English in British Columbia.

Rotenberg's experience highlights another quality that many believe helped them survive and served them well in later life: their capacity to develop a chameleon-like quality which enabled them to adapt quickly to changing conditions. Robert Krell believes that what helped the young people survive emotionally, then and now, is their extraordinary adaptability. Their ability to sense change, adapt readily to new surroundings, and to do what has been demanded of them, has lasted into adulthood. Likewise their ability to compartmentalize issues. Above all, what has struck Krell is their "considerable intellect in addition to a set of intuitive skills which are often staggering."

Greta Fischer offered another perspective based on her work with the young survivors in Montreal. The inner resources that had enabled them to survive as children became liabilities for some later in life, she believed. Their ability to adapt like a chameleon sometimes turned into confusion, loss of identity and alienation; those who had spent years living in forests, drifting from place to place, and trading on the black market were expected to stay in one place when they arrived in Canada. Reflex habits such as running away when demands were not met, or seeing the doppelgänger of an S.S. officer in every teacher or foreman were difficult to erase.

Despite the magnitude of the demands facing them, the child survivors quickly showed great skill for adjusting and integrating into Canadian life. The determination with which they worked to gain

Group of war orphans at baseball game, Winnipeg,
spring or summer, 1949.
Photo by Portigal & Wardle
Canadian Jewish Congress National Archives

control over their lives and succeed through their own efforts can be seen in the results of a follow-up survey done for Congress by Ben Lappin.[4] Two years after the last arrival in April 1951, less than 20 percent of the war orphans brought to Canada by Congress were in the care of social agencies—including boys and girls under sixteen years of age who were still at school.

Today, this type of success is seen as evidence of a quality which has gained the status of theory under the general heading of "resilience." It is most often applied in analysis of social outcomes among traumatized and disadvantaged children in contemporary society, but can also be used as a tool of historical analysis. In August 1995, psychologist John Sigal from the Jewish General Hospital in Montreal, presented a paper at the Annual Meeting of the American Psychological Association in which he noted irrefutable evidence for resilience among survivors and their families. He referred to a study done in 1982 by researchers Robinson and Hemmendinger who found that children who survived Buchenwald and were seen by their caretakers as either psychotic or psychopaths, thirty years later were found to have adjusted well.

What appears to be resilience in one area of functioning is not necessarily an indication of resilience in all areas. It is found where one would least expect it—among child survivors. In explaining this resilience Sigal concludes: "Endowment, temperament, or familial environmental factors that pre-dated the persecution can variously be invoked to explain these resilience-producing traits." He also refers to earlier studies which demonstrate that the post-Holocaust environment was much more predictive of the adult functioning of these children than the pre- or Holocaust events in their lives. Can this finding be interpreted as a further validation of the well-founded premises and application of Congress' Project?

Sigal finds it noteworthy that there are some 15,000 references—clinical and empirical—to adult survivors, but only a handful dealing with child survivors.

For children who had seen the worst the world can offer, the leap into the future in Canada made them feel, they say, that anything was possible. They felt bold and unafraid of taking risks. However, there were also those who were paralyzed by a profound sense of insecurity and shame about being a child of the Holocaust. Their fear of disclosure was born in part by the fear they perceived which some Canadians had—the fear that the survivor was a member of a different breed and best avoided. Their sense of loss interwoven with feeling like abandoned outsiders played such havoc with their self-esteem that it was almost impossible for them not to blame themselves for being unworthy. It is not lack of empathy with victims which makes people turn their backs when hearing about cruelty. More often than not it is because they are revolted, and have no idea about how to react. Stories of cruelty reduce people to silence. In his last dark meditation just before taking his own life, Primo Levi wrote of Holocaust survivors recalling variations of the same recurrent nightmare. "They had returned home and with passion and relief were describing their past sufferings, addressing themselves to a loved one. But they were not believed, or even listened to."

The majority of child survivors have never told their stories to anyone until recently. As children they were encouraged not to tell, but to lead normal lives and forget the past. In the youngsters' minds, as Dr. Krell has come to understand it, it is restated as, "Is it not time to forget your parents, your brothers and sisters?"

Allan Weiss, who established a successful business after starting out as a window salesman has no problem talking about his war years. "Maybe it's because I was so young when I went through it. You're on a roller coaster, and you don't know why you're rolling—you just go with the punches." But the thing that boggles the mind is "how was it possible for my father not to have known in 1944 what was happening, maybe 350 miles away in Auschwitz?"

Surely had my father known he would have tried to escape. And always on my mind is the question whether I could have helped him after we were taken to Auschwitz. It was he who saved my life. The Germans were looking for boys old enough to work but I was underage. My father insisted I show myself willing and I became one of the people responsible for bringing soup into the barracks. From time to time I was able to scrape a little bit extra. Could I have helped him live if I had found a way to give him some? I will always wonder.

For many survivors "memory is a two-edged sword." As Dr. Krell has written:

> Not to have memories deprives one of a connection to all those who loved and nurtured you as an infant and child. To have memories means never being free of the fear and dread of those horrible times. For example, one child survivor's only memory of his mother is being torn from her arms to safety while she is pushed onto a train for deportation and death. He never wants to forget his mother; he always wants to forget that train.[5]

The writer Aharon Appelfeld, also a child survivor wrote that "it was impossible to live after the Holocaust except by silencing memory. Memory became your enemy. You worked constantly to blunt it, to divert it, and to numb it as one numbs pain. This battle lasted for years. People learned how to live without memory the way one learns to live without a limb of one's body."[6]

Other people see memory as folding in upon itself like geologic layers of rock. The deeper strata sometimes re-appear on top and when this happens it flashes news from below. The passing years often trigger this cycle, stirring up the strata that once lay out of reach. Then the processing lens of memory re-selects what it places in the foreground and what it leaves in the background. As many child survivors of the Holocaust reach their fifties and sixties, buried memories often erupt in this way. For others a balanced life can be maintained only if the memories remain buried far out of reach of consciousness, as if a mist of time serves as a statute of limitations on the recall of things painful and wrong.

At the first Conference on Hidden Children convened in 1991 in New York City, it was noted that a proportionately large number of child survivors had chosen careers in the health and helping professions. Krell maintains that a primary objective of most survivors was to marry and have a family; to create their own home and replace the destroyed family. "And in addition to establishing a strong home and family life," he adds, "child survivors have found other ways of creating meaningful lives by becoming workers in the helping professions, supporting organizations devoted to the care of childen, and working for the Jewish community."What does this teach us about their adaptive capacities and coping strategies? And what can they teach us about what proved helpful, and what irrevelant and detrimental? To what degree did being received by fellow Jews contribute to their remarkable adaptation?

Regarding the manner in which some of the young people chose careers, Krell offers interesting insights:

> For the Jewish refugee child used to hiding, a variation on the theme was to hide by acquiring a skill recognized by all, but incompatible with being a refugee from the Holocaust. A great scholar of English, a talented athelete, an outstanding singer or actor—all objectives were sought to melt into society. Grief and memories remained private, skills and talent went public.[7]

Epilogue

It is no accident that Canada's Department of Immigration was grafted onto the Department of Mines and Resources. From its earliest days Canada has treated refugees and immigrants as a resource to be exploited economically, just as its natural resources are exploited. It is now common knowledge that this did not change when the Second World War broke out and hundreds of thousands of victims of Nazi terror were seeking escape from Germany.

The Canadian National Committee on Refugees, an independent, non-sectarian organization of Canadian citizens, working to promote a pro-refugee movement accurately read the mood of the country. Founded in 1938 with Senator Cairine Wilson as its moving spirit it was disbanded in 1948. In its efforts to bring about a change in government policy the organization knew how to strike at, or at least aim for, the right chords, and tailored its publicity and educational materials accordingly. In large, bold type it asks in a publication circulated in 1940, "Refugees: What Are We Going To Do About Them?" And then answers by assuaging public fears.

Refugees stimulate employment and create new industries. New processes, new patents, and new machinery have been brought to Canada by refugees. They will increase our Canadian manufacturing trade. Paint remover, seed cleaning, pulling and scratching flax and drying paprika are some of the new processes. Farmers can grow paprika now…Canada formerly imported 600,000 lbs. of paprika a year. Paprika is a food with a high vitamin C content.

Refugees...are working as research experts in Canadian laboratories...One is working on cancer causes, and another has produced an antidote for poison gas.

The widespread fear Canadians held about newcomers taking away jobs was further addressed by CNCR which demonstrated statistically that just the opposite would occur. "Refugees are creating employment for Canada. Two hundred Canadians found jobs in one firm established by a refugee, and there is another firm which employs about 500 and is expected to need 1,600 men when it runs at full capacity."

A year earlier, in the summer of 1939, the *Winnipeg Free Press* had done its part in trying to convince its readers how refugees brought new opportunities for Canadians. An editorial argued that "we are deliberately keeping out of this country men and women who would greatly add to our productive revenues. We are cutting off our nose to spite our face."

When Canada finally changed its immigration policy in 1947, selection was not based on the refugee's needs, but Canada's. The key which unlocked the door to Canada was self-interest—labour was needed to feed a rapidly expanding and industrializing economy. No preference was given to those longest in refugee camps or who had suffered most. Selection was based on a demonstrated successful adaptation and good health. Humanitarian considerations did not appear to enter into the selection process. David Matas, a Winnipeg lawyer with a special interest in refugee rights, spelled out the law of conduct when he wrote that "while an immigrant policy cannot be faulted for being geared to what is good for Canada, rather than what is good for refugees, a refugee policy should be humanitarian with its purpose to help refugees, not help Canada."[1]

Canada was not alone in following this policy, nor have things changed significantly since. According to the United Nations High Commissioner for Refugees (it succeeded the IRO in 1951), which holds the statutory responsibility for seeking permanent solutions for the problems of refugees, in 1995 only 10 of the world's 180 states accepts the obligation to accept resettlement cases on a regular basis. In many instances "countries have given priority not to the refugees with the most urgent needs, but to those who have the best potential for integration, who have some strategic value and who come from communities with strong domestic constituencies lobbying on their behalf." [2]

There was a time when the large-scale movement of refugees was regarded as a temporary phenomenon, the aftermath of either disaster or war. But we now recognize that these movements have become not only a defining feature of our times, but also a rising tide. Refugees, like the poor, seem destined to be with us always. The UNHCR states: "At few times in recent history have such large numbers of people in so many parts of the globe been obliged to leave their own countries and communities to seek safety elsewhere." The global refugee problem continues, and given world-wide political turmoil, will continue to confront the world with practical challenges and ethical dilemmas.

The UNHCR also maintains that more than half of the world's refugees are children and adolescents, and in some refugee situations, they constitute as high as 65 percent of the displaced population. Relative to these numbers, the War Orphans Project of 1947-1949 is insignificant in size; however, what it achieved and how it succeeded in reaching its goal is a remarkable accomplishment not only for its time but also in light of current research. In the context of the 1990s, and studied in retrospect, the policies and practices of the Project were based on a solid base of intelligent and thoughtful considerations that current research has shown to be fundamental for success.

As indicated earlier, efforts to do a follow-up study of the Jewish war orphans were not productive. However, it is my distinct impression, based on the people I met and those who were spoken about, that most have done exceptionally well. Although one hesitates to place the orphans who survived the Holocaust alongside other groups of refugees, I believe one can draw on some principles about the key components which have proven helpful to refugees learning to live and work in a new environment.

It is widely acknowledged by those working in the field that resettlement requires time; unfortunately most research has been limited to "snapshot" surveys and evaluations which do not follow the same refugees over several years. To rectify this lack Dr. Morton Beiser, presently Program Head of Culture, Community and Health Studies, Clarke Institute of Psychiatry and the Department of Psychiatry, University of Toronto, undertook a longitudinal research on refugee adaptation. It was his belief that "simply knowing that refugee resettlement is stressful offers little help in formulating policy or planning services."[3] His research aimed to identify the salient stresses which block adaptation, be they intolerable memories, social isolation, or structural characteristics of the new society.

Of paramount importance, Beiser demonstrated, is what happens to people after they enter the country of permanent asylum. This has a greater effect on their mental health during the first years of resettlement than what happened to them before.[4]

Furthermore, in a ten-year study of South East Asian refugees in Canada, Beiser found that popular theory introduced more than forty years ago postulating predictable stages of psychological adjustment "tells more about the appeal of formulas that seem to predict behaviour, than about resettlement."[5] Although migration and resettlement are undoubtedly stressful, it is the availability of social support and differences in personal resources which determine how well refugees fit in. Resettlement agencies now recognize that local ethnic communities who can help replace familial and social networks are essential for the mental health of refugees without family.

Fifty years ago the Canadian Jewish community embraced this concept unequivocally and found innovative ways to make it happen.

One wonders whether the Canadian government drew on the successes of the War Orphans Project when it designed a programme to assist refugees to adapt and become self-sufficient. The Host Program for Refugee Settlement, a Canada-wide pilot project funded by Employment and Immigration Canada in 1985, matches Canadian volunteers with refugee families and individuals in order to provide non-material assistance and guidance for one year. It began in London, Ontario in response to a large influx of Vietnamese refugees and by 1989 had expanded to eighteen projects across the country.

During the research for this book a dramatic and moving sequence invariably accompanied the closing of every meeting with the man or woman who had been a war orphan. It took a number of forms. On many occasions I would be shown, if any existed, the one or two precious photographs of themselves as children with their parents celebrating a happy event. At other times I would be invited to share their pride and pleasure in the photos of their children taken at graduation, a wedding ceremony, or other momentous events in life's passage. And of course, if grandparents, there were the happy faces of grandchildren to be admired. At other closings something quite different would occur.

On one occasion, although I was a complete stranger from out of town, I made a brief introductory phone call to someone I wanted to interview. I was welcomed with the warmth and hospitality usually reserved for favourite friends. Before exchanging goodbyes, in a confidential tone my host said, "I want to show you something." It was reassuring because I took it to mean I had passed a test. I could never stop myself from worrying whether I was *really* understanding what I heard, or whether it was even possible. It didn't help that I was told over and over again how no Canadian could possibly understand what they had gone through. I agree.

Abe studied my face with renewed concentration. One sign of false emotion on my part, I knew, would stop him in his steps. He asked me to follow him down the hall to where a sturdy walnut sideboard with three deep-set drawers stood facing the front door. Bending to open the bottom drawer, Abe drew carefully from its safe corner a small square piece of thick, tattered paper. He held it in the palm of his hand examining it, seemingly unaware for the moment that he had brought it out to show to me. He handled it as if it were a living thing. He peered at it from one angle, then turned it around to inspect it from another perspective, as if it might have changed shape or grown since he saw it last. When I looked at the piece of rough paper, turned brittle and wrinkled, its once-black letters and numbers grey with age, I realized that for Abe this was much more than an inanimate object. It was a cherished amulet that would never lose its lustre. Embedded within its cells, refracting the light like a sparkling diamond, was freedom.

It brought to mind the hundreds of sad stories I had heard and read over the years about how one's life could depend on getting *papers*: the succession of historical crises in Europe—the revolutions, the wars, the pogroms, the imprisonments—which forced people to flee for their lives. They had to have papers. My parents' and their *landsmen* told stories about their flight from Europe to Canada at the turn of the century. For that they too had to have papers. *Papers, papers, papers.* You had to have papers to leave a place and to get into a new one, and often just to be allowed to live. There were never enough papers for everyone who wanted them, and there were always people who could take your papers away and you might never be seen or heard from again.

I recalled as well the many photographs I had seen, taken in Europe prior to the outbreak of World War Two. Desperate parents, their babies cradled in their arms or their young children gripping their hands, or clinging to a skirt or pant leg, stood huddled together in block-long lines. They waited and waited, and hoped. They knew that their lives depended on being admitted into those imposing buildings where foreign embassies held the power to grant precious *papers*.

Accepting refugees is an act of compassion and, to paraphrase

Aristotle, a nation's greatness can be measured by its compassion. Opening the doors to refugees and welcoming them with openness and generosity encourages their dreams, and grants them the same hope of self-realization as the members of the host society would wish for themselves. The War Orphans Project exemplified this spirit.

Notes

CHAPTER ONE

1. Trudy Mitic Duivenvoorden and J.P. Leblanc, *Pier 21—The Gateway That Changed Canada* (Nova Scotia: Lancelot Press, 1988).

2. Canadian Jewish Congress National Archives Kg 01.

3. Sidney Katz, "The Redeemed Children," *Maclean's Magazine,* January 10, 1962.

CHAPTER TWO

1. Irving Abella and Harold Tropper, *None is Too Many* (Toronto: Lester & Orpen Dennys Ltd., 1982).

2. Cyril Levitt and William Shaffir, "The Swastika as Dramatic Symbol," *The Jews In Canada*, ed. Robert J. Brym, William Shaffir, Morton Weinfeld (Toronto: Oxford University Press, 1993).

3. Public Archives of Canada, IR, File 739325.

4. Abella, 118.

5. Memo written by Hayes to Bronfman on March 5, 1943. Canadian Jewish Congress Archives, U.J.R. file 231.

6. P.A.C., IR, file 376333.

7. P.A.C., R.G. 26, Vol. 120, file 3-26-1.

8. C.J.C. Archives.

9. Abella, 223.

10. P.A.C., Immigration Branch, RG Vol. 477, file 739325.

CHAPTER THREE

1. Patricia Rooke, *No Bleeding Heart: Charlotte Whitton, a Feminist on the Right* (U.B.C. Press, 1987).

2. P.A.C, Interim 64, Vol. 817, file 551-16.

3. Kenneth Begnell, *The Little Immigrants: The Orphans Who Came to Canada* (Macmillan, 1980).

4. Philip Bean and Joy Melville, *Lost Children of the Empire* (London: Unwin Hyman, 1989).

5. Bernard Figler, *Lillian and Archie Freiman* (Ottawa: Northern Printing, 1959).

6. A.D. Hart, ed., *The Jew in Canada* (1926).

7. David Rome, "The Morals of the Time," *The Immigrant Story* (Montreal: Canadian Jewish Archives, 1986.)

8. Benjamin Lappin, *The Redeemed Children* (Toronto: University of Toronto Press, 1963).

9. Ruth Tannenbaum, former Director of Youth Protection for Quebec, in an interview with the author.

10. Bagnell, *The Little Immigrants.*

11. C.J.C. Archives, file Ca.

12. Lappin, *The Redeemed Children.*

13. P.A.C. MG V86 Vol. 45.

14. Lappin.

15. Greta Fischer, former worker in the Reception Home, in an interview with the author.

16. P.A.C. V86 Vol. 46.

CHAPTER FOUR

1. C.J.C. Archives, file DA 4.

2. C.J.C. Archives, P86/10.

3. P.A.C. Interim 64, Vol. 817, file 551.

4. Patricia T. Rooke and R.L. Schnell, *Discarding the Asylum* (Lanham, MD: University Press of America, 1983).

5. C.J.C. Archives, DA 3.

6. Hayes' unpublished memoir, C.J.C. Archives.

7. Lappin.

8. Ibid.

CHAPTER FIVE

1. Gerald E. Dirks, *Canada's Refugee Policy* (Kingston and Montreal: McGill-Queens University Press, 1977).

2. Michael R. Marrus, *The Unwanted* (New York: Oxford University Press, 1985).

3. George Woodbridge, *UNRRA: The History of United Nations Relief and Rehabilitation Agency* (New York: Columbia University Press, 1950).

4. Greta Fischer, personal papers.

5. Canadian Jewish Congress Ontario Archive.

6. P.A.C. RG 26 Vol. 120.

7. Lottie Levinson in an interview with the author.

8. Ostry file in I.R.O. Congress National Archives and P.A.C. MG 30 C 184.

CHAPTER SEVEN

1. C.J.C. Archives.

2. Ibid.

3. Ibid.

4. Larry Rotenberg, "A Child Survivor/Psychiatrist's Personal Adaptation," *Journal of the American Academy of Child Psychiatry*, 24, 4:385-389, 1985.

5. P.A.C. MG 28 V86 Vol.46.

6. Deborah Dwork, *Children With a Star* (Yale University Press, 1991).

7. P.A.C. MG 30 C 152 Vol. 4.

8. Lappin.

9. Aharon Appelfeld, *Beyond Despair* (New York: Fromm International Publishing, 1994).

CHAPTER EIGHT

1. Lappin.

2. Ibid.

CHAPTER NINE

1. Robert Krell and Sarah Moskovitz, "Child Survivors of the Holocaust: Psychological Adaptations to Survival" *Israel Journal of Related Sciences*, Vol. 27 No.2 (1990).

2. William B. Helmreich, *Against All Odds* (New York: Simon & Schuster, 1992).

3. Larry Rotenberg, "A Child Survivor/Psychiatrist's Personal Adaptation," *Journal of the American Academy of Child Psychiatry*, 24 (1985), 4:385-389.

4. Ben Lappin, unpublished Progress Report on the War Orphan Study, Oct. 28, 1959. PAC MG 28 V86 Vol. 46.

5. Robert Krell, "Child Survivors of the Holocaust: Strategies of Adaptation Then and Now." Paper presented at the Joint Meeting of the American and Canadian Academies of Child Psychiatry, 1988.

6. Aharon Appelfeld, *Beyond Despair* (Fromm International Publishing Corp., 1994).

7. Robert Krell, "Children Who Survived the Holocaust: Strategies of Adaptation." Paper presented at the Canadian Academy of Child Psychiatrists, 1986.

EPILOGUE

1. C.J.C. Archives.

2. Abella, p.65.

3. David Matas, *Closing the Doors: The Failure of Refugee Protection*, (Toronto: Somerhill Press, 1989).

4. United Nations High Commissioner for Refugees, *The State of the World's Refugees* (Oxford University Press, 1955).

5. Howard Adelman, "The Mental Health of Refugees in Resettlement Countries," *Refugee Policy, Canada and the United States*, York University and Center for Migration Studies of New York (York Lanes Press, Toronto, 1991).

6. M. Beiser et al., "Catastrophic Stress and Factors Affecting Its

Consequences Among Southeast Asian Refugees," *Social Science and Medicine,* 28, 1989.

7. M. Beiser, "The Mental Health of Refugees in Resettlement Countries,"*Refugee Policy, Canada and the United States* (Toronto: York Lanes Press, 1991).